Dark Morning Star Rising

Gregory John

Marigold House

This book is dedicated

To my dear and loving wife, who has been a great support and has been instrumental in helping me complete this book,

and

To all who share in the blessed hope of Jesus' return, yet are in the dark about Satan's end-time deceptions that he is preparing to cast upon this world, including, if possible, God's elect.

"Watch ye therefore, and pray always, that ye may be accounted worthy to escape all these things that shall come to pass, and to stand before the Son of man."
Luke 21:36

Contents

Preface

Standing at the opposite poles of Christendom today are two peculiar peoples of faith. Each having their origins in the American expansion of the nineteenth century, they are now worldwide movements that are growing at a faster rate than most other Christian faiths. In the not-so-distant future, I believe that neither Christendom nor the world will be able to easily ignore either one of these peoples of faith or their "bi-polar" special messages for earth's inhabitants. To do so would be to ignore the prophetic significance of these two faiths and their teachings.

Who are these peculiar peoples of faith? *The Church of Jesus Christ of Latter-day Saints* (Mormons) and the *Seventh-day Adventists*.

As a student of Bible prophecy, I believe we are living in what the Bible prophet Daniel referred to as "the time of the end." I also believe it is crucial for God's people today to have a clear and wise understanding of the Bible's end-time prophecies. Failure to do so, I fear, will leave many captive to the enemy's subtle lies as well as vulnerable to his grand end-time deceptions that shall bring many to the awful place of perdition. Furthermore, I believe the prophetic books of Daniel and Revelation are open books to our understanding and, when correctly studied together, provide a great blessing and sound assurance to those who read, hear, and heed the things which are written in them.

As you read and examine this book, may the Holy Spirit of truth (not your personal feelings, religious experiences, or doctrinal beliefs) be your trustworthy guide. As for the acceptance of truth, it often passes through three stages: "First, it is ridiculed; second, it is violently opposed; and, third, it is accepted as self-evident" (Arthur Schopenhauer, 1788-1860).

As one watching and waiting for the Lord's return, I desire that you, the reader, will come to know and understand the biblical truths for this present time, so as to be wise and watchful for "the Son of man [Jesus] coming in the clouds of heaven with power and great glory" (Matthew 24:30).

"When religious prejudice is removed, the light of
Bible truth is revealed." Gregory John

Section I

Prophets and Prophecies

Chapter One

The Day of the Lord

"Blow ye the trumpet in Zion, and sound an alarm in my holy mountain: let all the inhabitants of the land tremble: for the day of the Lord cometh, for it is nigh at hand."
Joel 2:1

One of the most solemn and heart-stirring events predicted throughout the Holy Scriptures is the great and awful day of the Lord or the second coming of Jesus Christ. On that most glorious day when the Sun of righteousness shall break upon the dawn, every eye shall see Him, and as far as the east is from the west, the kingdoms of this world shall be no more.

For those watching and waiting for His promised return, this will be a great day of rejoicing: "Lo, this is our God; we have waited for him, and he will save us: this is the Lord; we have waited for him, we will be glad and rejoice in his salvation" (Isaiah 25:9). For the rest of the world, it will be a day of dread and terror as they call out to the mountains and rocks, "Fall on us, and hide us from the face of him that sitteth on the throne, and from the wrath of the Lamb: for the great day of his wrath is come; and who shall be able to stand?" (Revelation 6:16-17).

The world today is no more prepared for Jesus' promised second coming than it was for His first coming when He came in the flesh almost 2,000 years ago. "He was in the world, and the world was made by him, and the world knew him not. He came unto his own, and his own received him not" (John 1:10-11). Like the wise Magi who carefully studied the sacred Scriptures and discerned the time of Christ's first coming, God's watchmen today continue to search the sacred Scriptures to discern the signs of the times.

As a fellow watchman, I believe that Bible prophecy in the light of history not only reveals to us that Jesus' second coming is close at hand, but also sheds light on Satan's counterfeits and end-time deceptions that will take place before His return. Furthermore, I believe that shortly before the time of Jesus' return, there will be a great spiritual awakening (see Revelation 18:1-4). It may be much like the spiritual awakening that occurred in early nineteenth-century America, later termed "The Second Great Awakening."[1]

The 1820s and 1830s fostered many evangelical revivals, the organization of Bible and missionary societies, and the growth of various social and health reform movements. It was also during this time that both The Church of Jesus Christ of Latter-day Saints (Mormon movement) and the Millerite "Advent" movement found their early beginnings in western New York State—one proclaiming another testament of Jesus Christ and the other proclaiming the soon coming of Jesus Christ.

Many Americans saw these sweeping revivals, temperance movements, and expanding Bible and missionary societies as outward signs pointing to the dawning of a new era (millennium) of spiritual enlightenment and restoration. This expectation was later termed "millennial fever." The postmillennialists were expecting Christ's return at the end of this blissful millennium, whereas the premillennialists believed that Christ's return would usher in the anticipated millennium.

Among the most noted millennial movements, the Millerite movement[2] got its name from a farmer turned preacher named William Miller. The firstborn of sixteen children, William, Jr., started life in the town of Pittsfield, Massachusetts, on February 15, 1782. When he was four, his family moved to a farm just south of Lake Champlain in Low Hampton, New York, where he spent his adolescent years. Having only a rural education, Miller, through the goodwill of some of the learned men in his community, began to further his education by borrowing and reading as many books as he could get his hands on.

In 1803, at age 21, Miller married Lucy P. Smith and soon afterwards took up farming near her hometown of Poultney, Vermont. Having an insatiable appetite for knowledge, Miller often frequented Poultney's public library, where he got to know and befriend some of the more learned men in the community. Though he had been brought up believing in God and the Bible, Miller's spiritual beliefs were eventually reshaped by the influences of his more educated friends, who held to a deistic view of the world. Deism teaches that God created the world and its natural laws but plays no active role in its function or the personal welfare of mankind.

After his military service as a captain in the War of 1812, Miller relocated his family to Low Hampton, where he bought a piece of land, built a house, and was planning to live out the remainder of his days in the bliss of being an American farmer. Unbeknownst to him, Providence had a different direction for the remainder of his life. Before too long, Miller's Low Hampton utopia began to falter and sway under his deistic views, which gave him no hope beyond the grave.

> Annihilation was a cold and chilling thought, and accountability was sure destruction to all. The heavens were as brass over my head, and the earth as iron under my feet. Eternity—what was it? And death—why was it? The more I reasoned, the further I was from demonstration. The more I thought, the more scattered were my conclusions. I tried to stop thinking, but my thoughts would not be controlled. I was truly wretched, but did not understand the cause. I murmured and complained, but knew not of whom. I knew that there was a wrong, but knew not how or where to find the right. I mourned, but without hope.[3]

Remembering his miraculous survival without injury in the battle of Plattsburg, Miller began to wrestle with his former biblical beliefs in God. It was this unexplainable event on the battlefield that led William Miller's soul to finally find rest in God's assurance, peace, and personal love for him in His Son—the Savior, Jesus Christ.

After his conversion experience, Miller joined the Low Hampton Baptist church, yet he was hard pressed to fully accept the Bible as God's revelation to man. Knowing that he had taunted others for entertaining a blind faith in the Bible, Miller removed from his mind any preconceived notions about the Bible and began to make a full and methodical study of the books of the Bible using as his guide a Bible concordance and the tested principle of allowing Scripture to be its own expositor. By 1818, almost two years into his studies, Miller had become convinced that the Word of God could be safely trusted. "I was thus satisfied that the Bible is a system of revealed truths, so clearly and simply given that the wayfaring man, though a fool, need not err therein."[4]

His studies also led him to believe that the popular postmillennial view of a temporal millennium of peace upon the earth prior to Christ's return was in direct violation of what the Scriptures plainly taught. Miller's studies of the prophetic book of Daniel, especially Daniel's timeline prophecies, led him to believe that Christ's return was close at hand and that the earth (commonly thought of at the time as a sanctuary) was soon to be cleansed with holy fire by the consuming glory of Christ's appearing. "Unto 2,300 days; then shall the sanctuary be cleansed" (Daniel 8:14).

In August of 1831, some fifteen years after starting his Bible study, William Miller finally acted upon his distressing conviction to go and tell the world of its danger.

> With the solemn conviction that such momentous events were predicted in the Scriptures to be fulfilled in so short a space of time, the question came home to me with mighty power regarding my duty to the world, in view of the evidence that had affected my own mind.[5]

Having halfheartedly entered into a covenant with God, Miller reasoned with God, "If I should have an invitation to speak publicly in any place, I will go and tell them what I find in the Bible about the Lord's coming."[6] Thinking that no invitation would ever come to a lowly farmer, he quickly felt that his burden had been lifted. Yet as Providence would have it, his covenant with the Lord was met that very same day with the invitation brought to his doorstep to come and share his biblical viewpoints on the second advent of Jesus Christ with the Dresden Baptist church.

Now left without excuse, Miller quickly found himself taking refuge in a nearby grove of trees, where he wrestled with God in prayer, asking to be released from his promise. In the end, William Miller surrendered his will to God and emerged from the maple grove with peace in his heart and a message to preach to anyone who would listen.

In the immediate years following his first invitation to preach, Miller and his Advent message were openly welcomed by many ministers in an effort to bring spiritual revival within their congregations as well as attract new converts. As the time grew closer to Miller's predicted year of Christ's coming (March 21, 1843, to March 21, 1844),[7] both his message and his Adventist followers increasingly became the subject of ridicule and prejudice among the clergy and parishioners of the various Protestant sects. Joseph Smith, the prophet and leader of the Mormon restoration movement, also publicly rejected Miller's predictions: "Were I going to prophesy, I would say the end [of the world] would not come in 1844, 5, or 6, or in forty years. There are those of the rising generation who shall not taste death till Christ comes."[8]

Many who were receptive to the Advent message found themselves either expelled from their church congregations or silenced by the threats of expulsion. In the years just prior to 1844, the Millerite believers moved out of the churches and into tent meetings (adapted from the Methodist camp meetings) as a means of evangelism and giving Bible studies to the masses. It is estimated that as many as 500,000 people attended the 125 Millerite tent meetings that were held from 1842 to 1844.

In March 1844, Joseph Smith again prophesied that Miller's prediction of Christ's coming in that same year would fail:

> But I will take the responsibility upon myself to prophesy in the name of the Lord, that Christ will not come this year [1844], as Father Miller has prophesied, for we have seen the bow [rainbow]; and I also prophesy, in the name of the Lord, that Christ will not come in forty years; and if God ever spoke by my mouth, He will not come in that length of time. Brethren, when you go home, write this down, that it may be remembered.[9]

When the predicted time period of March 1843-44 passed by without Christ's return, many, including Miller himself, found their high hopes dashed upon the rocks. For the Millerites who had not lost faith in the movement, August 12, 1844, marked a time of needed revival. On that day Millerite advocate Samuel S. Snow presented at the Exeter, New Hampshire, tent meeting his reasoning for Christ's return to be on the Jewish Day of Atonement (the tenth day of the seventh month), which was reckoned to occur on October 22, 1844. Snow surmised that the cleansing of the sanctuary (thought to be the earth) at Christ's coming was to be the antitype fulfillment to the type or symbolic cleansing of the ancient earthly sanctuary on the Day of Atonement or Day of Judgment for the Israelites.

Out of the Exeter tent meeting revival came forth the "midnight cry" proclaimed to the world: "Behold the bridegroom cometh; go ye out to meet him" (Matthew 25:6). As a result of this renewed urgency to prepare a people for the Lord's coming, it is estimated that as many as 50,000 left their churches to join the Millerite movement. In the weeks prior to October 22, many left their jobs, put off the harvest of their crops, and set aside the mundane and leisure activities of life so as to prepare and warn as many people as possible before the Lord's imminent return.

Miller himself, who had never set a specific date for Christ's return, was at first opposed to this new movement, but in the weeks prior to October 22, 1844, he accepted it with the reservation that the specific day of October 22 might or might not be the day of the Lord's glorious return to earth. In a letter written on October 6, 1844, to his friend and Adventist colleague Joshua Himes, he stated,

> I see a glory in the seventh month which I never saw before. Although the Lord had shown me the typical bearing of the seventh month, one year and a half ago, yet I did not realize the force of the types. Now, blessed be the name of the Lord, I see a beauty, a harmony, and an agreement in the Scriptures, for which I have long prayed, but did not see until today. Thank the Lord, O my soul. Let Brother Snow, Brother Storrs, and others, be blessed for their instrumentality in opening my eyes. I am almost home. Glory! Glory! Glory! . . . If Christ does not come within 20 or 25 days, I shall feel twice the disappointment I did in the spring.[10]

For William Miller and the multitudes who had wholeheartedly believed in his message and who were caught up in the rapture of the Midnight Cry message, October 22, 1844, marked the day of most bitter disappointment when Jesus Christ did not come as had been anticipated. Those who had joined the movement mostly out of fear soon renounced their faith in the Second Advent movement and mocked those who still clung to Miller's message. Some lost faith in religion altogether, whereas others sought to find an answer to their heartfelt disappointment.

Joseph Smith and the Mormon restoration movement never set a date, but Joseph did allude to Christ's second coming around the years 1890-91, a prediction which history has long since dispelled.

> It was the will of God that those who went to Zion, with a determination to lay down their lives, if necessary, should be ordained to the ministry, and go forth to prune the vineyard for the last time, or the coming of the Lord, which was nigh—even fifty-six years should wind up the scene. —*Address given February 14, 1835*[11]

> I was once praying very earnestly to know the time of the coming of the Son of Man, when I heard a voice repeat the following: Joseph, my son, if thou livest until thou art eighty-five years old, thou shalt see the face of the Son of Man; therefore let this suffice, and trouble me no more on this matter. I was left thus, without being able to decide whether this coming referred to the beginning of the millennium or to some previous appearing, or whether I should die and thus see his face. I believe the coming of the Son of Man will not be any sooner than that time.[12]

In the first statement, 56 years after 1835 would be 1891. As for Smith's second statement, he was born on December 23, 1805; therefore, had he lived a full 85 years, his 85th birthday would have been on December 23, 1890. However, Joseph was not clear on whether this event would be the second coming, a personal appearance of Christ to him, or his death. Joseph mentions seeing the face of the Son of Man on at least two occasions in his life (Doctrine and Covenants 76:20-24; 110:2-10).

In looking back at the history of the Millerite movement, it is not hard to see that the spirit and fervor that attended the movement not only stirred up many hearts to anticipate Jesus' return, but also brought ridicule and strong opposition from Protestant ministers and parishioners who had to openly defend nonbiblical teachings such as postmillennialism that they held in common with Roman Catholicism.[13] Will the same spirit of fervor and animosity attend the great and final spiritual awakening? Time will tell! As Christians, it is important to be ready for Jesus' coming, but let us not put our blessed hope of His return on specific dates or even a specific year, which is both speculative and a dangerous precedent.

Summary:

In the early nineteenth century, the United States of America witnessed a spiritual awakening or what was later termed "the Second Great Awakening." It was during this time of spiritual awakening that both The Church of Jesus Christ of Latter-day Saints (Mormons) and the Millerite "Advent" movement found their early beginnings in western New York State. For the Mormon movement it marked a time of restoration and a more complete gospel (the Book of Mormon) pointing to Jesus Christ and His return. For William Miller and the Millerite movement it marked a time of spiritual revival, Christian reform, and preparation for the anticipated soon return of Jesus Christ.

> *"Watch therefore: for ye know not what hour your Lord doth come. . . . Therefore be ye also ready: for in such an hour as ye think not the Son of man cometh."*
> *Matthew 24:42-44*

Notes:

1. The first spiritual awakening in America occurred during the mid-eighteenth century in the then English-controlled colonies.

2. The Millerites came out of the "Burned-Over District" of western central New York, an area where many spiritual revivals and reform movements took root, thus leaving the area exhausted or "burned over" of new converts.

3. Sylvester Bliss, *Memoirs of William Miller* (Boston, MA: Joshua Himes, 1853), 65

4. Bliss, *Memoirs of William Miller*, 70

5. Bliss, *Memoirs of William Miller*, 81

6. Bliss, *Memoirs of William Miller*, 97

7. These dates marked the Jewish calendar year of 1843.

8. Joseph Smith and George Albert Smith, *History of the Church of Jesus Christ of Latter-Day Saints*, vol. 5 (Salt Lake City, UT: Deseret Book, 1950), 33
https://byustudies.byu.edu/content/volume-5-chapter-17

9. Smith, *History of the Church*, vol. 6, 254
https://byustudies.byu.edu/content/volume-6-chapter-10

10. Jerome L. Clark, *1844: Religious Movements*, vol. 1 (Nashville, TN: Southern Publishing Assoc., 1968), 48

11. Smith, *History of the Church*, vol. 2, 182
https://byustudies.byu.edu/content/volume-2-chapter-13

12. *The Doctrine and Covenants of the Church of Jesus Christ of Latter-Day Saints* (Salt Lake City, UT: The Church of Jesus Christ of Latter-day Saints, 1981), section 130:14-17; see an alternate and extended version in *History of the Church*, vol. 5, 336

13. St. Augustine in his fifth-century book, *The City of God*, laid much of the framework for the ideology of postmillennialism in nineteenth-century America.

Chapter Two

The Seer of All Man's Days

"But of that day and hour knoweth no man, no, not the angels of heaven, but my Father only." Matthew 24:36

In the days of Noah, God saw that the wickedness of man was so great that his thoughts and intentions were full of evil. "And God said unto Noah, The end of all flesh is come before me; for the earth is filled with violence through them; and, behold, I will destroy them with the earth" (Genesis 6:13). God declared to Noah not only man's future, but also the time allotted: "And the Lord said, My spirit shall not always strive with man, for that he also is flesh: yet his days shall be an hundred and twenty years" (Genesis 6:3).

God, who created man, takes no pleasure in his death or destruction. "As I live, saith the Lord God, I have no pleasure in the death of the wicked; but that the wicked turn from his way and live" (Ezekiel 33:11). Yet as He forewarned Noah, the destruction of the wicked came when "the world that then was, being overflowed with water, perished" (2 Peter 3:6). If God could reveal to Noah the impending destruction of the then-known world, then He surely can reveal, through His chosen prophets, the future of our world today. "But the heavens and the earth, which are now, by the same word are kept in store, reserved unto fire against the day of judgment and perdition of ungodly men" (2 Peter 3:7).

God's calling of prophets has always been for the divine purpose of revealing His intentions and will for man's eternal wellbeing. Essentially, "the Lord God does nothing unless He reveals His secret counsel to His servants the prophets" (Amos 3:7, NASB). This is the sure word of prophecy. God will not leave His true followers groping in the dark for understanding as to the prophetic hour in which they live.

The Old Testament prophets were often given the unpopular task of condemning men's sinfulness in the face of God's judgment to come. History points this out with the proud and obstinate city of Jerusalem, which repeatedly ignored God's warnings and slew His prophets: "O Jerusalem, Jerusalem, thou that killest the prophets, and stonest them which are sent unto thee, how often would I have gathered thy children together, even as a hen gathereth her chickens under her wings, and ye would not! Behold, your house is left unto you desolate" (Matthew 23:37-38).

To contradict God's spokesmen, Satan has always raised up false prophets for the purpose of turning men's minds away from the truth and God's warnings. During the time of God's prophet Jeremiah, there were other supposed prophets living in Jerusalem—all claiming to speak for the Lord. "Ye shall not see the sword, neither shall ye have famine; but I [the Lord] will give you assured peace in this place," they announced. But the Lord said to Jeremiah, "The prophets prophesy lies in my name: I sent them not, neither have I commanded them, neither spake unto them: they prophesy unto you a false vision and divination, and a thing of nought, and the deceit of their heart" (Jeremiah 14:13-14). With the destruction of Jerusalem in 598 BC, it became evident that these false prophets had lied!

So how can anyone know with certainty which, if any, prophetic messengers to believe? The Scriptures tells us, "To the law and to the testimony: if they speak not according to this word, it is because there is no light in them" (Isaiah 8:20). In other words, a true prophet or ministering spirit (angelic being) will always speak in harmony with the straight testimony of God's Word, which never changes (Numbers 23:19, Malachi 3:6) nor passes away with the seasons of time (Psalm 111:7-8; Isaiah 40:8). Otherwise the messenger and their message are to be rightly rejected.

The Lord God, who is the creator and sustainer of all things in the heavens above and on the earth below—He alone is God and the great Seer of all man's days in the past, present, and future, and He alone reveals His secret counsel to His servants the prophets.

Summary:

Can anyone accurately foresee and foretell the events and outcomes of tomorrow? With perfect accuracy God Himself can, and He surely told His prophet Noah! As for our future, God alone knows all, sees all, and reveals to His bondservants, the prophets, that which is destined to come, including the passing away of this fallen world not by a deluge of water, but with an all-consuming and unquenchable fire.

"But the day of the Lord will come as a thief in the night;
in the which the heavens shall pass away with a great
noise, and the elements shall melt with fervent heat,
the earth also and the works that are therein
shall be burned up." 2 Peter 3:10

Chapter Three

The Sure Word of Prophecy

*"How that by revelation he made known unto me the
mystery; (…whereby, when ye read, ye may understand
my knowledge in the mystery of Christ) which in other
ages was not made known unto the sons of men, as it
is now revealed unto his holy apostles and prophets
by the Spirit." Ephesians 3:3-5*

Many Christians living today believe that modern-day revelations from God do not exist. One of the main Scripture references for this premise is found in the book of Hebrews, which states, "God, who at sundry times and in divers manners spake in time past unto the fathers by the prophets, hath in these last days spoken unto us by his Son" (Hebrews 1:1-2). In other words, Jesus' testimony, which we have in the New Testament Scriptures, is the endpoint of all prophecy.

In seeking a biblical basis for the continuance of prophecy and revelation, there are four lines of evidence that shouldn't be ignored: (1) the testimony of Joel; (2) the testimony of Jesus; (3) the testimony of Paul, and (4) the testimony of John the Revelator.

1) The testimony of Joel

A prominent testimony for the continuance of the gift of prophecy is found in Joel 2:28-29, which states, "And it shall come to pass *afterward*, that I will pour out my spirit upon all flesh: and your sons and your daughters shall prophesy, your old men shall dream dreams, your young men shall see visions: and also upon the servants and upon the handmaids in those days will I pour out my spirit" (emphasis supplied).

The apostle Peter, as well as many other early Christians, saw Joel's prophecy as being fulfilled on the Day of Pentecost. "But this is that which was spoken by the prophet Joel; And it shall come to pass *in the last days*, saith God, I will pour out my Spirit upon all flesh: and your sons and your daughters shall prophesy" (Acts 2:16-17, emphasis supplied). While it is true that Peter identified the outpouring of the Holy Spirit (the gift of tongues) with Joel's prophecy, we must remember that Joel's prophecy points to those living in the last days just prior to Jesus' return: "And I will shew wonders in the heavens and in the earth, blood, and fire, and pillars of smoke. The sun shall be turned into darkness, and the moon into blood, before the great and terrible day of the Lord come" (Joel 2:30-31).

When examining Joel's prophecy, we find that it is set in the context of ancient Israel's yearly agricultural cycle, which included three main harvests. The first was the spring or grain harvest of barley and wheat, whereas the other two were the wine (grape) and oil (olive) harvests of late summer and early autumn. In the Hebrew agricultural year, which began in the autumn, the former or early rainy season (autumn) helped prepare the soil for the time of sowing wheat and barley seed, whereas the latter rainy season (spring) helped ripen the grain for the time of harvest. "And he [the Lord your God] will cause to come down for you the rain, the former rain, and the latter rain in the first month.[1] And the floors shall be full of wheat, and the vats shall overflow with wine and oil" (Joel 2:23-24).

With the outpouring of the Holy Spirit on the Day of Pentecost (the Feast of Harvest), Peter believed that the latter rain had come, and along with it, the soon fulfillment of the great commission: "And this gospel of the kingdom shall be preached in all the world for a witness unto all nations; and then shall the end come" (Matthew 24:14). Peter's misunderstanding may have stemmed from the belief that the early or former rain was symbolic of Jesus' 3½ years of sowing the gospel seed of the kingdom to come. Given that nearly 2,000 years have passed since the Day of Pentecost, it is evident that the Day of Pentecost marked the beginning and not the approaching end of the great commission.

Knowing that Peter witnessed the early outpouring of the Holy Spirit (speaking in tongues), which prepared the way for many to join the early apostolic church, we too can expect the latter outpouring of the Holy Spirit (prophesying, dreams, and visions) to help prepare the way for the great and final harvest depicted in the book of Revelation (Revelation 14:14-16).

2) The testimony of Jesus

Jesus makes no mention of the gift of prophecy as far as the church is concerned, but He does warn His followers of false Christs and false prophets showing great signs and wonders prior to His return (Matthew 24:24-27). Satan's counterfeit to the gift of prophecy has always been marked by false signs and wonders. "And Moses and Aaron went in unto Pharaoh, and they did so as the Lord had commanded: and Aaron cast down his rod before Pharaoh, and before his servants, and it became a serpent. Then Pharaoh also called the wise men and the sorcerers: now the magicians of Egypt, they also did in like manner with their enchantments. For they cast down every man his rod, and they became serpents: but Aaron's rod swallowed up their rods" (Exodus 7:10-12).

Knowing that true and false miracle-working prophets fought for supremacy prior to Egypt's plagues, it stands to reason that true and false miracle-working prophets will once again struggle for supremacy prior to earth's seven last plagues (Revelation 15-16).

3) The testimony of Paul

In his first epistle to the church in Corinth, the apostle Paul addresses the Holy Spirit's role in endowing spiritual gifts within the body of believers (the church). These diverse spiritual gifts, which include the gift of prophecy, are "for the perfecting of the saints, for the work of the ministry, [and] for the edifying of the body of Christ" (Ephesians 4:12). The question, then, to ask is, "Are all the spiritual gifts, including the gift of prophecy, to remain with the church until the time of completion of the great gospel commission?" Paul's answer is "Yes": "Till we all come in unity of the faith, and of the knowledge of the Son of God, unto the perfect man, unto the measure of the stature of the fullness of Christ" (Ephesians 4:13).

Furthermore, when it comes to the purpose of the gifts themselves, Paul tells us that "he that speaketh in an unknown tongue edifieth himself; but he that prophesieth edifieth the church. . . . Even so ye, forasmuch as ye are zealous of spiritual gifts, seek that ye may excel to the edifying of the church" (1 Corinthians 14:4-12). If the gift of prophecy is for the "edification," "exhortation," and "comfort" of the saints (1 Corinthians 14:3), then there is no reason or scriptural basis for the gift to be absent from the church. To suggest or believe otherwise would reflect the Laodicean Church's mindset: "I am rich, and increased with goods, and have need of nothing" (Revelation 3:17).

Therefore we would do well to heed Paul's words of admonition to the church at Corinth: "Grace be unto you, and peace, from God our Father, and from the Lord Jesus Christ. . . . That in everything ye are enriched by him, in all utterance, and in all knowledge; even as the testimony of Christ was confirmed in you: *so that ye come behind in no gift*; waiting for the coming of our Lord Jesus Christ" (1 Corinthians 1:3-7, emphasis supplied).

4) The testimony of John the Revelator

John the Revelator tells us that the gift of prophecy is to remain with God's remnant or latter-day people: "And the dragon [Satan] was wroth with the woman, and went to make war with the remnant of her seed, which keep the commandments of God, and have the testimony of Jesus Christ" (Revelation 12:17). "For the testimony of Jesus is the spirit of prophecy" (Revelation 19:10).

When comparing scripture with scripture, it is evident that the testimony of Jesus and the spirit of prophecy are synonymous with each other:

Revelation 19:10	Revelation 22:9
"And he said unto me, See thou do it not: I am thy fellowservant"	"Then saith he unto me, See thou do it not: for I am thy fellowservant"
"and of thy brethren that have the testimony of Jesus"	"and of thy brethren the prophets"

When it comes to the question of the continuance of the gift of prophecy in these latter days of the Christian dispensation, the Word of God clearly states that every matter or word may be established on the testimony of two or more witnesses (Matthew 18:16). Therefore we have the assurance of four witnesses who all testify that prophecy will not be done away with until the return of Jesus.

Summary:

Throughout history, God has set apart for His divine purposes select men and women to be His holy messengers (prophets) so as to guide, instruct, reprove, warn, and console His people. The gifts of the Spirit, which include prophecy, are for the perfecting of the saints, the work of ministry, and the edification of the church body. As for the gift of prophecy itself, it is to remain with God's remnant people who in the latter days keep the commandments of God and have the testimony of Jesus Christ, which the Scriptures tell us is the spirit of prophecy (Revelation 12:17; 19:10).

> *"We have also a more sure word of prophecy; whereunto*
> *ye do well that ye take heed, as unto a light that shineth*
> *in a dark place, until the day dawn, and the day star*
> *arise in your hearts." 2 Peter 1:19*

Notes:

1. The first month of the Jewish year falls in March-April.

Chapter Four

The Principles of Prophetic Study

"Blessed is he that readeth, and they that hear the words
of this prophecy, and keep those things which are written
therein: for the time is at hand." Revelation 1:3

Throughout history, men have looked in wonderment upon the celestial bodies—the sun, moon, and stars, including our solar system's starry bright planets[1]—as deities or as sacred oracles for predicting the future. But what does the Lord God, who made the heavens and all their hosts of glory, have to say about seeking knowledge from or paying homage to these celestial bodies?

"If there be found among you . . . man or woman, that hath . . . gone and served other gods, and worshipped them, either the sun, or moon, or any of the host of heaven, which I have not commanded . . . then shalt thou bring forth that man or that woman, which have committed that wicked thing, unto the gates . . . and shalt stone them with stones, till they die" (Deuteronomy 17:2-5).

Furthermore, should we be seeking wisdom and knowledge from psychics or fortunetellers who claim to have a seeing eye into the future?

"There shall not be found among you any one that maketh his son or his daughter to pass through the fire, or that useth divination [fortunetelling], or an observer of the times [astrologer], or an enchanter, or a witch, or a charmer, or a consulter with familiar spirits [medium or channeler], or a wizard, or a necromancer [sorcerer]. For all that do these things are an abomination unto the Lord: and because of these abominations the Lord thy God doth drive them out from before thee" (Deuteronomy 18:10-12).

God's sacred Word distinctly tells us that the doers and seekers of such things as mentioned are an abomination unto the Lord of hosts. Therefore, let us seek to know the counsel of the Lord God our Creator, whose wisdom and knowledge stretch not only as far as the east is from the west, but as high as the heavens above. "The heavens declare the glory of God; and the firmament sheweth his handywork. Day unto day uttereth speech, and night unto night sheweth knowledge" (Psalm 19:1-2).

As for the book of Revelation ("the Revelation of Jesus Christ"), it not only reveals to us God's foreknowledge of earth's history and end-time events, but also foretells the restoration of all things, including a new earth, new heavens, and a new Jerusalem. Sadly, most Christians today scarcely seek to read or understand this all-important prophetic book. Is this what the Lord God would want from His people living in the last days? Surely not!

When it comes to the study of apocalyptic or end-time prophecy as outlined in the book of Revelation, there are three distinct schools of interpretation: (1) Preterism, (2) Futurism, and (3) Historicism.

Preterism[2] (from the Latin word *praeter*, meaning "past") seeks to show that most if not all of John the Revelator's prophecies were fulfilled during the early centuries of the Christian church.

Futurism[3] proposes that the bulk of John the Revelator's prophecies are yet to be fulfilled within a brief time period just prior to Christ's second coming. Modern-day Christians who believe in a secret rapture followed by a seven-year period of tribulation upon the earth most closely subscribe to the Jesuit school of Futurism.

Historicism, or "continuous historical" interpretation, views John the Revelator's prophecies as unfolding along a historical timeline that begins with the prophet John's time and ends with God's kingdom of glory being set up upon the new earth.

When it comes to interpreting apocalyptic Bible prophecy, I as a historicist used the following eight principles (keys) of interpretation when writing this book.

Principle 1: All of Scripture

Second Timothy 3:16 is the foundation from which all prophecy is to be studied. "All scripture [Old and New Testament] is given by inspiration of God, and is profitable for doctrine, for reproof, for correction, for instruction in righteousness."

In using this principle, first gather together all scripture texts on the subject matter being studied. Second, using a Bible concordance, examine key words and phrases within the texts so as to know the true and proper meaning in the original language in which they were written. A Bible concordance is a valuable study tool for examining and interpreting translated words or phrases that were originally penned in the languages of Hebrew and Aramaic (Old Testament writings) or Greek (New Testament writings). Third, after evaluating their meaning and context, retain the Bible texts that are found to be relevant to the subject matter being studied.

An example of this study principle can be found with the English word "times," which in the Old Testament writings may have different meanings depending on the word from which it is translated.

"And he shall speak great words against the most High, and shall wear out the saints of the most High, and think to change **times** (1) and laws: and they shall be given into his hand until a **time** (2) and **times** (2) and the dividing of **time** (2)." Daniel 7:25

1) Times = Hebrew word *zeman*, meaning an appointed time or season.
2) Times = Hebrew word *iddan*, meaning a set time or year (see also Daniel 4:23-26).

Based on this second meaning of the word "times," as well as other Bible passages referring to this same prophecy (see Chapter 8), the latter part of this verse signifies "a time [1 year] and times [2 years] and the dividing of time [1/2 year]."

Principle 2: Scripture as Its Own Expositor

Let scripture interpret scripture. This principle, which is sometimes called "Isaiah's Principle," is found in Isaiah 28:9-10: "Whom shall he teach knowledge? and whom shall he make to understand doctrine? . . . For precept must be upon precept . . . ; line upon line . . . ; here a little, and there a little." When using this "scripture upon scripture" principle, it is important to remember that it is not any one verse but precept upon precept and line upon line that helps bring about and bridge understanding.

An example of this principle is found in the Bible's own interpretation of the word "sleep":

"And they went on stoning Stephen as he called upon the Lord and said, 'Lord Jesus, receive my spirit!' And falling on his knees, he cried out with a loud voice, 'Lord, do not hold this sin against them!' And having said this, he fell **asleep**." Acts 7:59-60, NASB

"Our friend Lazarus **sleepeth**; but I go, that I may awaken him out of sleep. . . . Then said Jesus unto them plainly, Lazarus is dead." John 11:11-14

"So David **slept** with his fathers, and was buried in the city of David." 1 Kings 2:10

"But man dieth, and wasteth away; yea, man giveth up the ghost, and where is he? As the waters fail from the sea, and the flood decayeth and drieth up: so man lieth down, and riseth not: till the heavens be no more, they shall not awake, nor be raised out of their **sleep**." Job 14:10-12

Principle 3: Symbolism

All scripture in Bible prophecy should be taken literally, unless it defies nature (e.g., a leopard with four heads and four wings) or there is a justifiable reason to believe that its meaning is figurative or symbolic. When trying to determine the literal or figurative meaning of a word or phrase in Scripture, first look for other scriptures that may identify and give further explanation as to its literal or figurative meaning.

An example of this principle shows the phrase "many waters" in Revelation 17 to be figurative:

"Come hither; I will shew unto thee the judgment of the great whore that sitteth upon **many waters**: with whom the kings of the earth have committed fornication, and the inhabitants of the earth have been made drunk with the wine of her fornication." Revelation 17:1-2

"And he saith unto me, The **waters** which thou sawest, where the whore sitteth, are **peoples**, and **multitudes**, and **nations**, and **tongues**." Revelation 17:15

Another example of this principle shows the word "fire" in Revelation 13:13 to be literal:

"And he doeth great wonders, so that he makes **fire** come down from **heaven** on the earth in the sight of men." Revelation 13:13

Applying principle 1 (All Scripture) to the words "fire" and "heaven," there are 22 verses found in the Bible that have the words "fire" and "heaven" or "heavens" in the same sentence. When comparing Revelation 13:13 with the other 21 Bible verses, two of which are found in the book of Revelation (Revelation 10:1, 20:9), the word "fire" in all 21 verses is clearly seen as being literal fire. Therefore there is just reason to believe that the fire seen coming down from heaven in Revelation 13:13 is also literal fire.

Principle 4: Year-Day
The timeline prophecies found in the books of Daniel and Revelation all follow the same principle of one prophetic day being equal to one literal year—a 360-day lunar calendar year. Several examples of this principle may be found in Old Testament.

"After the number of the days in which ye searched the land, even forty days, each day for a year, shall ye bear your iniquities, even forty years, and ye shall know my breach of promise." Numbers 14:34

"For I have laid upon thee the years of their iniquity, according to the number of the days, three hundred and ninety days: so shalt thou bear the iniquity of the house of Israel. And when thou hast accomplished them, lie again on thy right side, and thou shalt bear the iniquity of the house of Judah forty days: I have appointed thee each day for a year." Ezekiel 4:5-6

Principle 5: Repeat and Enlarge

The main points of a vision or parable are sometimes repeated and enlarged (magnified) by other more descriptive scriptures. An example of this principle can be found in the prophetic book of Daniel, where the visions of the prophet Daniel (Daniel 7 and 8) repeat and enlarge upon King Nebuchadnezzar's visionary dream (Daniel 2).

Kingdoms	Daniel 2	Daniel 7	Daniel 8
Babylon (605-539 BC)	Head of gold (verses 32, 38)	Lion with wings (verse 4)	Not mentioned; Daniel's vision pertains to the future when Babylon is no more
Media-Persia (539-331 BC)	Chest of silver (verses 32, 39)	Bear with one shoulder higher than the other (verse 5)	Ram with one horn longer than the other (verses 3, 20)
Greece (331-168 BC)	Thighs of brass (verses 32, 39)	Leopard with 4 heads (verse 6)	Goat whose large horn is broken off and replaced by 4 horns (verses 5, 8, 21, 22)
Rome (168 BC-AD 476)	Legs of iron (verses 33, 40)	A dreadful and terrifying beast with 10 horns; 3 of its horns are later replaced by a little horn (verses 7, 8, 23, 24)	Little horn power that replaces the goat's 4 remaining horns (verses 9-12, 23-25)

Principle 6: Type-Antitype

In the Old Testament of the Bible there are many types or patterns of things that have their antitype or fulfillment in the New Testament. A Bible type is essentially a historical truth (person, place, event, or thing) that foreshadows or points forward to a counterpart (antitype). A Bible antitype is usually broader in meaning (amplified), proving to be the "body" which was foreshadowed by the type. The key to understanding this principle can be found in the unity of the Scriptures themselves.

An example of this principle is the sanctuary or tabernacle of God. In the Old Testament, Moses is called by God to construct a sanctuary: "And let them make me a sanctuary; that I may dwell among them. According to all that I shew thee, after the pattern of the tabernacle, and the pattern of all the instruments thereof, even so shall ye make it" (Exodus 25:8-9). In the New Testament we find that the earthly sanctuary was patterned after the heavenly sanctuary. The book of Hebrews refers to Jesus as "a minister of the sanctuary, and of the true tabernacle, which the Lord pitched, and not man" (Hebrews 8:2). "For Christ is not entered into the holy places made with hands, which are the figures of the true; but into heaven itself, now to appear in the presence of God for us" (Hebrews 9:24). In the beauty of this principle, we see that the earthly sanctuary was a type or pattern pointing forward to its perfect antitype, the heavenly sanctuary, where Jesus Christ as our great High Priest is now ministering as man's intercessor before God.

Principle 7: Historical Application and Examination

When it comes to history affirming Bible prophecy, the first and primary application is to examine the prophecy in relation to the time period in which it was written. By attempting to answer the 5W's (Who, What, Where, When, and Why), you will be better able to determine whether or not the prophecy has already had its fulfillment in history.

If there is reason to believe that the prophecy has not yet been fulfilled, then the next application is to examine whether or not the prophecy has any set conditions attached to it. If so, then as a conditional prophecy it may have already had its place in history as being unfulfilled.

An example of an unfulfilled conditional prophecy was when the prophet Jonah walked through the wicked city of Nineveh prophesying, "Yet forty days, and Nineveh shall be overthrown" (Jonah 3:4). When the people of Nineveh quickly heeded the prophet's doomsday message and repented of their wicked ways, God in His love, mercy, and grace abstained from pouring out His wrath upon the city. Thus the prophet's words were prevented from coming to pass (see Jeremiah 18:7-8).

The third and final application is to examine the Bible prophecy in the light of known historical events or corroborated facts. If the prophecy can be linked to a particular event or fact without violating the meaning of any words, figures, or symbols and without distorting the context of the prophet's message, then the prophecy may be considered validated by history. An example of history validating prophecy can be found in the book of Daniel, where history affirms what the prophet Daniel predicted regarding the rise and fall of four earthly kingdoms: Babylon, Media-Persia, Greece, and Rome.

As for the application and examination of a particular prophecy having dual or multiple fulfillments in history, it has NO place in this or any other principle used in this book.

Principle 8: The Thessalonian Test (1 Thess. 5:20-21)

A) "Despise not prophesying."

When it comes to a new theory being presented as truth, one should always be cautious but, at the same time, not too hasty in rejecting it or having the Laodicean mindset that "I am rich [in understanding], and increased with goods, and have need of nothing [more]" (Revelation 3:17). To maintain such an attitude shall surely bind the mind, close the ears, and shut the eyes to the advancement of truth.

B) "Prove all things."

When it comes to examining or testing a new theory, one must always weigh every point of controversy with the straight testimony of God's Word. To allow one's personal beliefs, feelings, culture, or even the spirit of prophecy to be the measuring stick of truth is to make the Word of God the interpretation and not the interpreter of truth (principle 2). In other words, if it fits your schema of knowledge and understanding and is supported by your formed beliefs, feelings, or religious experiences, then it must be a correct interpretation—whereas in reality it may be a square peg (one's own interpretation) fitting into a round hole (the Bible's interpretation).

C) "Hold fast that which is good."

When it comes to accepting or rejecting a theory (new or old), all opinion, without prejudice or fear, must rest upon the Word of God. If a theory is found to be in harmony with the Word of God, doesn't violate the principles mentioned, and can be supported by history (principle 7), then consider it to be truth unless proven otherwise.

Without exception, when this or any other principle is being applied, one must always approach God's Word with a humble and teachable spirit, along with the spiritual keys of faith and prayer in hand. In doing so, one may unlock the mysteries of God's Word. "And all things, whatsoever ye shall ask in prayer, believing, ye shall receive" (Matthew 21:22). "And ye shall know the truth, and the truth shall make you free" (John 8:32).

Summary:

Throughout history, man has sought knowledge and wisdom from the things of creation instead of from the all-knowing, all-seeing, and all-wise God who created the heavens, earth, and every living thing. The occult practices of astrology, fortunetelling, channeling of spirits, etc., descend "not from above, but [are] earthly, sensual, [and] devilish" (James 3:15). In contrast, "the path of the just [God's people] is as the shining light [God's Word],[4] that shineth more and more unto the perfect day" (Proverbs 4:18).

When it comes to the revelations of God given to man, the book of Revelation or "the Revelation of Jesus Christ" is to be viewed as an open book of understanding to those who read, hear, and heed the words therein. There are basically three schools of interpretation for the prophecies of the book of Revelation: Preterism, Futurism, and Historicism. Yet when it comes to the prophecies of Revelation, only historicism provides us with the blessing of assurance for the things yet to come, by way of the prophetic waymarks of the things already fulfilled in history.

"And he saith unto me, Seal not the sayings of the
prophecy of this book: for the time is at hand."
Revelation 22:10

Notes:

1. Our solar system's planets are sometimes referred to as "wandering stars" due to their orbital movement.

2. Preterism was proposed by the Jesuit Alcazar (AD 1614) in counteraction to the Protestant Reformation.

3. Futurism was proposed by the Jesuit Ribera (AD 1591) in counteraction to the Protestant Reformation.

4. Psalm 119:105: "Thy word is a lamp unto my feet, and a light unto my path."

Section II

Kings and Kingdoms

Chapter Five

The Lamb of God

*"And I beheld, and I heard the voice of many angels
. . . saying with a loud voice, Worthy is the Lamb that
was slain to receive power, and riches, and wisdom,
and strength, and honour, and glory, and blessing."*
Revelation 5:11-12

Throughout the book of Revelation, the most significant and central figure is the Lamb of God, who is mentioned no less than twenty-seven times. In John the Revelator's visions, the focal point of activity surrounding the Lamb is the act of praise and worship among the heavenly host and those redeemed by the blood of the Lamb, which reveals the great awe and joy all can experience in having a personal love relationship with the Lamb!

In Revelation 5, it is the Lamb as **man's redeemer and atoning sacrifice** who is seen taking from Him who sits upon the throne a book of mysteries and breaking open its seven seals. In response to the Lamb's selfless sacrifice, heaven's twenty-four elders are seen bowed down and singing, "Thou art worthy to take the book, and to open the seals thereof: for thou wast slain, and hast redeemed us to God by thy blood out of every kindred, and tongue, and people, and nation; and hast made us unto our God kings and priests: and we shall reign on the earth" (Revelation 5:9-10).

In Chapter 7, it is the Lamb as **man's loving and caring shepherd** who is seen surrounded by a great multitude who have come out of the great tribulation and washed their robes in the blood of the Lamb. "And they cried with a loud voice, saying, Salvation to our God which sitteth upon the throne, and unto the Lamb" (Revelation 7:10).

In Chapter 14, it is the Lamb as **man's victor over death** who is seen standing on Mount Zion with the 144,000 redeemed unto God and to the Lamb. "And they sung as it were a new song before the throne, and before the four beasts, and the elders: and no man could learn that song but the hundred and forty and four thousand, which were redeemed from the earth" (Revelation 14:3).

In Chapters 15 and 17, it is the Lamb as **man's lord and triumphant king** who is seen waging war in favor of His chosen and faithful servants, who neither worship the beast and his image nor receive the mark of his name. "And they sing the song of Moses the servant of God, and the song of the Lamb, saying, Great and marvelous are thy works, Lord God Almighty; just and true are thy ways, thou King of saints. Who shall not fear thee, O Lord, and glorify thy name? for thou only art holy: for all nations shall come and worship before thee; for thy judgments are made manifest" (Revelation 15:3-4).

In Chapters 18, 19, and 20, it is the Lamb as **man's just and true judge** who is seen passing judgment on the great harlot city as well as on those whose names are not written in the Lamb's book of life. "Alas, alas that great city Babylon, that mighty city! for in one hour is thy judgment come" (Revelation 18:10). "Alleluia; salvation, and glory, and honour, and power, unto the Lord our God: for true and righteous are his judgments: for he hath judged the great whore, which did corrupt the earth with her fornication, and hath avenged the blood of his servants at her hand" (Revelation 19:1-2). "And I saw the dead, small and great, stand before God; and the books were opened: and another book was opened, which is the book of life: and the dead were judged out of those things which were written in the books, according to their works" (Revelation 20:12).

In Chapter 21, it is the Lamb as **man's mediator and high priest** who is seen standing in the beauty of holiness (God's presence) and who is the perfect reflection of God's glorious image. "And I saw no temple therein: for the Lord God Almighty and the Lamb are the temple of it. And the city had no need of the sun, neither of the moon, to shine in it: for the glory of God did lighten it, and the Lamb is the light thereof" (Revelation 21:22-23).

In Chapter 22, it is the Lamb as **man's eternal wellspring of life** who is seen at the right hand of God and from whom freely flows the fountain of life to those who thirst after righteousness. "And he shewed me a pure river of water of life, clear as crystal, proceeding out of the throne of God and of the Lamb. . . . And on either side of the river [of life], was there the tree of life, which bare twelve manner of fruits, and yielded her fruit every month: and the leaves of the tree [of life] were for the healing of the nations" (Revelation 22:1-2).

The Lamb's Identity

1) Man's redeemer and atoning sacrifice

Since the time sin entered our world through Adam and Eve, there has been a sacrificial lamb. For Adam and Eve, it was the promise of a Savior which was typified in the death of an animal to provide a covering of animal skins. For the Israelites, it was the atoning blood of a slain lamb on their doorposts that protected them during the last plague (death of the firstborn) in Egypt. In commemoration of God's deliverance from the bondage of slavery, the annual Passover feast symbolized man's deliverance from the bondage of sin and death. For early and latter-day Christians today, it was and is the sacrificial and Passover Lamb (Jesus) who, as man's Redeemer, selflessly gave up His life on Calvary's cross and whose innocent blood both atones for our sins and protects us from the second death.

"The next day John seeth Jesus coming unto him, and saith, Behold the Lamb of God, which taketh away the sin of the world" (John 1:29).

2) Man's loving and caring shepherd

Any good and faithful shepherd will always meet the needs of the sheep under his watchful care and safekeeping. If one of his sheep should go missing or be in harm's way, he will not forsake or abandon it. Surely goodness (green pastures and refreshing waters) and mercy (unmerited love) shall follow his flock all the days of their lives.

Jesus is the Good Shepherd who watches over and cares for us as His children. If one of us should wander away from the family of God or be preyed upon by the enemy (Satan), He promises to never leave or forsake us. The riches of His glory and grace are without measure to those who love and obey him. Surely His goodness and mercy shall always be with those who call upon His name and find their resting place in Him.

"The Lord is my shepherd; I shall not want. He maketh me lie down in green pastures: he leadeth me beside the still waters. He restoreth my soul: he leadeth me in the paths of righteousness for his name's sake. Yea, though I walk through the valley of the shadow of death, I will fear no evil: for thou art with me; thy rod and thy staff they comfort me. Thou preparest a table before me in the presence of mine enemies: thou anointest my head with oil; my cup runneth over. Surely goodness and mercy shall follow me all the days of my life: and I will dwell in the house of the Lord for ever" (Psalm 23:1-6).

3) Man's victor over death

Sin is man's mortal wound that ends in death. For all have sinned (committed lawlessness)[1] and fall short of the glory of God, but thanks be to God, who in His infinite mercy and foresight made a way for our salvation before sin existed. Because of the indescribable gift and promise of His only begotten Son (Jesus), we may know that He who died and rose again from the grave is He who now holds the keys of hell and death, and in Him is the resurrection power over death.

"O death, where is thy sting? O grave, where is thy victory? The sting of death is sin; and the strength of sin is the law. But thanks be to God, which giveth us the victory through our Lord Jesus Christ" (1 Corinthians 15:55-57).

4) Man's lord and triumphant king

In the great and epic war between Christ and Satan, man's salvation was won at Calvary's cross. Knowing that his time is short, Satan in his enmity against God continues to make war with His people. In the last days, this will culminate with the beast from the bottomless pit and the kings of the earth making war with the Lamb and those who "by the blood of the Lamb and by the word of their testimony" shrink not from death (Revelation 12:11). In the final battle between good and evil, the battle of Armageddon, Jesus shall come wearing the victor's crown as the King of glory and the great conqueror over all the enemies of God.

"And I saw, and behold a white horse: and he that sat on him had a bow; and a crown was given to him: and he went forth conquering, and to conquer" (Revelation 6:2).

"And he was clothed with a vesture dipped in blood: and his name is called The Word of God. . . . And he hath on his vesture and on his thigh a name written, KING OF KINGS AND LORD OF LORDS" (Revelation 19:13-16).

5) Man's just and true judge

King Solomon in his wisdom and understanding said, "Fear God, and keep his commandments: for this is the whole duty of man. For God shall bring every work into judgment, with every secret thing, whether it be good, or whether it be evil" (Ecclesiastes 12:13-14). This is good counsel, knowing that everyone, including Satan and his confederate angels, will one day be judged. Those found written in the Lamb's book of life will be protected from both earth's last plagues and the final judgment that will come upon those who can't claim the blood of the Lamb (Jesus) for the propitiation of their sins.

"And I saw the dead, small and great, stand before God; and the books were opened: and another book was opened, which is the book of life: and the dead were judged out of those things which were written in the books, according to their works. And the sea gave up the dead which were in it; and death and hell delivered up the dead which were in them: and they were judged every man according to their works. And death and hell were cast into the lake of fire. This is the second death. And whosoever was not found written in the [Lamb's] book of life was cast into the lake of fire" (Revelation 20:12-15).

6) Man's mediator and high priest

From the time of Moses until Jesus' death on the cross, God's veiled presence dwelt with men in the holy of holies in the earthly temple. The temple's high priest was the mediator between God and His people.

Jesus' shed blood, an atonement for sin, made a new and living way for us to be able to come into the holy presence of God through Jesus as our heavenly High Priest and Mediator. In the city of God (New Jerusalem), there will be no need of a temple or mediator, for the transfigured and holy bodies of the saints will be able to stand in the unveiled and glorious presence of God and of the Lamb.

"For Christ is not entered into the holy places made with hands, which are the figures of the true; but into heaven itself, now to appear in the presence of God for us" (Hebrews 9:24).

"Having therefore, brethren, boldness to enter into the holiest by the blood of Jesus, by a new and living way, which he hath consecrated for us, through the veil, that is to say, his flesh; and having an high priest over the house of God; let us draw near with a true heart in full assurance of faith" (Hebrews 10:19-22).

"But ye are come unto mount Sion [Zion], and unto the city of the living God, the heavenly Jerusalem, . . . to the general assembly and church of the firstborn, which are written in heaven, and to God the Judge of all, and to the spirits of just men made perfect, and to Jesus the mediator of the new covenant, and to the blood of sprinkling, that speaketh better things than that of Abel" (Hebrews 12:22-24).

7) Man's eternal wellspring of life
Without the replenishing of water, a person can live for only a few days. Blessed are they who thirst after righteousness, for they shall drink freely from the wellspring of living water "proceeding out of the throne of God and of the Lamb" (Revelation 22:1).

"But whosoever drinketh of the water that I [Jesus] shall give him shall never thirst; but the water that I shall give him shall be in him a well of water springing up into everlasting life" (John 4:14).

The Lamb who was slain and now lives forevermore is none other than man's Redeemer—Jesus Christ. As victor over sin, Sheol (death), and Satan, He is worthy of all worship. As the king of glory, He alone is worthy of the sevenfold coronation of "power, and riches, and wisdom, and strength, and honour, and glory, and blessing" (Revelation 5:12).

Summary:

The Lamb who was slain and who is seen standing in the midst of God's throne is Jesus Christ, who alone is worthy of all praise, honor, and worship. His innocent blood shed on Calvary's cross not only met sin's demand and paid the price for our salvation but made a way for all things to be restored as God had originally ordained. Today, as the redeemed sons and daughters of God, we can look forward to a rich and glorious inheritance to come. Amen!

> *"He was oppressed, and he was afflicted, yet he opened not his mouth: he is brought as a lamb to the slaughter, and as a sheep before her shearers is dumb, so he openeth not his mouth. . . . Yet it pleased the Lord to bruise him; he hath put him to grief: when thou shalt make his soul an offering for sin, he shall see his seed, he shall prolong his days, and the pleasure of the Lord shall prosper in his hand. He shall see of the travail of his soul, and shall be satisfied: by his knowledge shall my righteous servant justify many; for he shall bear their iniquities." Isaiah 53:5-11*

Notes:

1. The Bible's definition of sin: "Whosoever committeth sin transgresseth also the law: for sin is the transgression of the law" (1 John 3:4).

Chapter Six

The Dragon, the Woman, and Her Child

"And there appeared a great wonder in heaven: a woman clothed with the sun, and the moon under her feet, and upon her head a crown of twelve stars. . . . And there appeared another wonder in heaven; and behold a great red dragon having seven heads and ten horns, and seven crowns upon his heads. And his tail drew the third part of the stars of heaven, and did cast them to the earth: and the dragon stood before the woman which was ready to be delivered, for to devour her child as soon as it was born." Revelation 12:1-4

John the Revelator, while imprisoned upon the rocky island of Patmos in the Aegean Sea, saw in wonderment a great red dragon standing in the presence of a pregnant woman adorned with the hosts of heaven (sun, moon, and stars). As he watched, the dragon poured out his fierce wrath upon the woman and her precious child, who was to rule over all the nations.

John's vision of the woman in Revelation 12 is widely believed to be symbolic, yet interpretations vary among the Christian sects. Roman Catholics see the woman as representing the Virgin Mary. Latter-day Saints (Mormons) claim that the woman symbolizes the kingdom of

God on earth, which in essence is their church restored upon the earth today. For many Protestants and evangelicals, the woman is symbolic of God's people. Historically she represents first Israel, who brought forth the Christ Child, and then, after Christ's ascension to heaven, she represents the Christian church, which is sometimes referred to as "spiritual Israel."

From a historicist point of view, the woman of Revelation 12 may well represent the kingdom of heaven on earth: before Adam's fall, now, and after the restoration of all things. As for her radiant glories (sun, moon, and stars), they may symbolize the varying hosts of heaven (God the Father, Jesus, and the angelic beings), as well as man's inherent glory both before the fall and after the glorious resurrection unto life eternal.

The Transitional Stages of the Kingdom of Heaven on Earth	
That was before Adam's fall	A kingdom of glory, where heaven and the newly created earth were united as one (Genesis 1:26-28)
That is after Jesus' resurrection	A kingdom of grace on the reclaimed earth today, uniting fallen men with heaven through the Savior, Jesus Christ (Revelation 5:8-10; Hebrews 4:14-16)
That is to come after death and Hades are swallowed up in the lake of fire	A kingdom of glory on the new (restored) earth, where both heaven and earth are to be forever united as one (Revelation 21:1-7)

Whatever your belief, there is no divergence of opinion that the woman is the one who in fulfillment of Genesis 3:15 brings forth the promised Christ Child.

While in vision, John saw something else most peculiar: a great red dragon having seven heads and ten horns, and on its heads seven crowns. Its action of sweeping away with its tail one third of the stars of heaven and its evil desire to devour the woman's child show it to be in direct conflict with the hosts of heaven. "And there was war in heaven: Michael and his angels fought against the dragon; and the dragon fought and his angels, and prevailed not; neither was their place found any more in heaven. And the great dragon was cast out, that old serpent, called the Devil, and Satan, which deceiveth the whole world: he was cast out into the earth, and his angels were cast out with him" (Revelation 12:7-9).

The dragon surely represents Lucifer, who by exalting himself first rebelled against God and thereafter planted the seeds of rebellion in one third of the angelic hosts. Having no longer a place in heaven, both Satan and his confederacy of sympathizing angels were cast out and hurled to the earth. "How art thou fallen from heaven, O Lucifer, son of the morning! how art thou cut down to the ground, which didst weaken the nations! For thou hast said in thine heart, I will ascend into heaven, I will exalt my throne above the stars of God: I will sit also upon the mount of the congregation, in the sides of the north: I will ascend above the heights of the clouds; I will be like the most High" (Isaiah 14:12-14).

The name Lucifer is translated in some modern Bible versions as "morning star." Once a glorious and highly admired angelic being, he is now a fallen and dark morning star.

Realizing the awful consequences of his unyielding rebellion, and filled with enmity towards God, the arch-rebel worked out a plan to counteract God's purpose and plan for our newly created world. Having access to God's crowning glories of creation, Adam and Eve, the serpent of old capitalized upon his devilish plan by sowing in Eve's mind the same subtle lie that he had first perpetrated in heaven: "Ye shall be as gods" (Genesis 3:5).

Subject to the same divine law and having the same free moral agency as the angelic hosts, Adam and Eve both chose to disobey God's command, and in doing so they entered into the same controversy that was first initiated in heaven by doubting God's love, wisdom, and eternal goodness. As victims of Satan's snare, and now subject to the awful consequences of their own rebellion, the fallen pair were soon met with God's love and mercy in the hope-filled promise of a Savior: "And I will put enmity between thee [Satan] and the woman, and between thy seed and her seed; it [Jesus] shall bruise thy head, and thou shalt bruise his heel" (Genesis 3:15).

Hoping to make void God's promise, Satan first attempted through his own seed (the children of wrath) to devour the woman's man child—Jesus, the promised Messiah. Seeing the Christ Child as a threat to his earthly throne, King Herod quickly ordered the killing of every male child two and under in and around the city of Bethlehem, where the Messiah was prophesied to be born. Having failed to devour God's promised Son, Satan then turned to the human agency of corrupt religious orders (Sadducees and Pharisees), who viewed Jesus as a threat to their priesthood authority over the Jewish people. After a mock trial, under the pretext of threats of insurrection, Roman governor Pontius Pilate submitted to their evil desires and demands and quickly ordered Jesus' death by crucifixion (Mark 15:10-15).

Even after Satan's expulsion from his heavenly home in Zion, his true character and malevolent desires were not fully recognized by the angelic hosts until the time of Jesus' death. The Savior's spilled blood at Calvary's cross not only marked the fulfillment of Genesis 3:15 but forever removed any sympathy for Satan, as well as the shadow of doubt that Satan had cast upon God's sovereignty and the perfection of His law, which is as just, true, and never-ending as is His love for our fallen world. "For God so loved the world, that he gave his only begotten Son, that whosoever believeth in him should not perish, but have everlasting life. For God sent not his Son into the world to condemn the world; but that the world through him might be saved" (John 3:16-17).

After Jesus' resurrection and ascension into heaven, where He is now the legitimate ruler of our world, Satan in his great fury went on the warpath (Revelation 12:13). In AD 70, through the agency of Rome, Satan destroyed the beautiful walls and palaces of Jerusalem, trampled down her holy sanctuary, and devoured much of her human host.

Seen as a type[1] of the heavenly city and its host, Jerusalem and her seed (God's people) were made the special subject of Satan's wrath and persecution not only by way of Rome, but also through the agency of another little horn power in the image of Rome,[2] which would trample upon God's Word and His heavenly sanctuary and would seek to devour His people, the persecuted Christians during the medieval Dark Ages.

God's people down through the ages have by faith persevered through the fiery trials and tribulations of life even unto death, thus overcoming the devil and his persecuting seed. In the latter days, the same will hold true with the remnant of the woman's seed, "which keep the commandments of God, and have the testimony of Jesus Christ" (Revelation 12:17). They too must endure Satan's fury and persecution until the end. "And they overcame him [Satan] because of the blood of the Lamb and because of the word of their testimony, and they did not love their life even to death" (Revelation 12:11, NASB).

The great spiritual conflict of the ages, which began in heaven and later found a foothold on the earth, not only reveals Satan's self-centered and malevolent desires to raise up his own kingdom but even more so reveals Jesus' self-sacrificing and benevolent love in laying down His heavenly crown and earthly life for lost humanity—a stark dichotomy between all that is good and evil. In the end when the mystery of God is finished, it shall be declared from heaven above, "The kingdoms of this world are become the kingdoms of our Lord, and of His Christ; and he shall reign for ever and ever" (Revelation 11:15).

Summary:

There was war in heaven! Michael and his angels fought with the dragon (Satan) and his angels. Having profaned their sanctuary home in heaven, the dragon and a third of the angels were cast down like lightning to the earth. Filled with great wrath and malice towards God, Satan drew our world into the controversy by way of deception. When Satan usurped Adam and Eve's dominion, both man and nature were placed under the bondage of sin and its penalty of death. Satan's triumph was soon met with God's promise of man's redemption as well as Satan's damnation (Genesis 3:15). Despite Satan's defeat and mortal blow at the cross of Calvary—the fulfillment of Genesis 3:15—he continues to show his great wrath and malice towards God, His kingdom, and His people, all the while knowing that his time upon this earth is short.

"And the dragon was wroth with the woman, and went to make war with the remnant of her seed, which keep the commandments of God, and have the testimony of Jesus Christ." Revelation 12:17

Notes:

1. See prophetic principle 6 in Chapter 4.
2. See Chapter 8 of this book for further explanation.

Chapter Seven

The Five Kingdoms

"Again, the devil taketh him [Jesus] up into an exceeding high mountain, and sheweth him all the kingdoms of the world, and the glory of them; and saith unto him, All these things will I give thee, if thou wilt fall down and worship me." Matthew 4:8-9

Satan, as the prince of darkness and first member of the dark trinity (Revelation 16:13-14), once held sway over four worldly kingdoms, each of which were in conflict with God's kingdom. As for the identity of these four temporal kingdoms, the book of Daniel through a series of prophetic visions and interpretations reveals to us what history has proven to be true. It also shows us that there is a God in heaven who knows all and who reveals to His servants (prophets) that which is sure to take place.

The first mention of these four earthly kingdoms is found in Daniel 2, where the God of heaven and earth reveals to the prophet Daniel not only the hidden visionary dream of a Babylonian king, but also its prophetic meaning.

King Nebuchadnezzar's Vision:
"Thou, O king, sawest, and behold a great image. . . . This image's head was of fine gold, his breast and his arms of silver, his belly and thighs of brass, his legs of iron, his feet part of iron and part of clay" (Daniel 2:31-33).

Daniel's Interpretation:

"Thou, O king, art a king of kings: for the God of heaven hath given thee a kingdom, power, and strength, and glory. . . . Thou art this head of gold. And after thee shall arise another kingdom inferior to thee, and another third kingdom of brass, which shall bear rule over all the earth. And the fourth kingdom shall be strong as iron: forasmuch as iron breaketh in pieces and subdueth all things. . . . And whereas thou sawest the feet and toes, part of potters' clay, and part of iron, the kingdom shall be divided. . . . So the kingdom shall be partly strong, and partly broken. . . . And in the days of these kings shall the God of heaven set up a kingdom [a stone cut out of the mountain without hands], which shall never be destroyed: and the kingdom shall not be left to other people, but it shall break in pieces and consume all these kingdoms, and it shall stand forever" (Daniel 2:37-44).

Daniel 7 repeats and enlarges upon King Nebuchadnezzar's dream and interpretation with the vision of four great beasts coming up out of a stormy sea.

Daniel's Vision:

"Behold, the four winds of the heaven strove upon the great sea. And four great beasts came up from the sea, diverse one from another" (Daniel 7:2-3).

"The first [beast] was **like a lion**, and had eagle's wings" (Daniel 7:4).

"A second **like a bear**, and it raised up itself on one side, and it had three ribs in the mouth of it" (Daniel 7:5).

"And lo another, **like a leopard**, which had upon the back of it four wings of a fowl; the beast had also four heads" (Daniel 7:6).

"And behold a fourth beast, dreadful and terrible, and strong exceedingly; and it had great iron teeth: it devoured and brake in pieces, and stamped the residue with the feet of it: and **it was diverse from all the beasts that were before it**; and it had ten horns" (Daniel 7:7).

Gabriel's Interpretation:

"These great beasts, which are four, are four kings, which shall arise out of the earth" (Daniel 7:17). The angel Gabriel further describes the fourth beast: "The fourth beast shall be the fourth kingdom upon earth" (Daniel 7:23).

History's Identification of the First Three Kingdoms

First Kingdom: Babylon—a lion with eagle's wings

"When the great [Assyrian] empire began to decline, Babylon rose for the last time. Media and Persia were equally ready to throw off the Assyrian yoke, and at length the allied armies of Cyaxares and the father of Nebuchadnezzar captured and destroyed the capital of the Eastern world. Babylon now rapidly succeeded to that proud position so long held by Nineveh. Under Nebuchadnezzar she acquired the power forfeited by her rival. The bounds of the city were extended; buildings of extraordinary size and magnificence were erected; her victorious armies conquered Syria and Palestine, and penetrated into Egypt. Her commerce, too, had now spread far and wide, from the east to the west, and she became a land of traffic and a city of merchants."[1]

"Israel is a scattered sheep; the lions have driven him away: first the king of Assyria hath devoured him; and last this Nebuchadnezzar king of Babylon has broken his bones" (Jeremiah 50:17).

Second Kingdom: Media-Persia—a bear with one shoulder higher than the other

"The Persian empire was created within the space of a single generation by a series of conquests that followed one another with a rapidity scarcely equalled except by Alexander. . . . The defeat of Astyages the Mede in 549 B.C. and of Croesus the Lydian in 546, the capture of Babylon in 538 and the conquest of Egypt in 525, gave the Persian empire within thirty years an extent exceeding that ever obtained by the greatest of monarchs of Mesopotamia or the Nile valley, and consequently greater than that of any earlier empire west of China."[2]

"The new state, the nucleus of the greater empire which [King]

Cyrus was yet to create and [King] Darius to solidify, consisted of the Medes and Persians; the greater empire itself, in the words of Darius, 'of Persia and Media and the other lands.'"[3]

Third Kingdom: Greece—a leopard with four heads and four wings

"In a declaration of war against Persia, Alexander took his army of about 40,000 soldiers and crossed the Hellespont in 334 B.C.E. With the help of his flying cavalry, as well as stout phalanxes of Macedonian hoplites (heavy infantry), Alexander dealt a crushing defeat to the army of King Darius III at the battle of Issus in 333 B.C.E. Alexander then proceeded to advance deep into the Persian realm, claiming Persian lands and booty for himself and his troops."[4]

"Only a month or two later he [Alexander] defeated Darius the Persian King at Issus (333 B.C.). Darius escaped, but Alexander was able to turn south and take control of Phoenicia and Egypt. From there he made an extraordinary expedition and cut west through the desert to the oracle of Zeus Ammon. . . . Thus encouraged, he marched north and east into Mesopotamia, where at Gaugamela (331 B.C.) he defeated Darius again, this time decisively. The Persian Empire, which had been a threat to the Greeks for more than 200 years, was now in the hands of Alexander."[5]

"Alexander the Great (356–323 BC) died suddenly at the age of 32, leaving no apparent heir or appointed successor. Some 40 years of internecine conflict followed his death, as leading generals and members of Alexander's family vied to control different parts of the vast empire he had built. The Battle of Ipsus, fought in Phrygia, Asia Minor (present-day Turkey) in 301 BC between rival successors, resulted in the empire's irrevocable dissolution. . . . Four main kingdoms . . . emerged after the battle. . . . The kingdom of Cassander (circa 358–297 BC), consisted of Macedonia, most of Greece, and parts of Thrace. The kingdom of Lysimachus (circa 361–281 BC), included Lydia, Ionia, Phrygia, and other parts of present-day Turkey. The kingdom of Seleucus (died 281 BC; later the Seleucid Empire), comprised present-day Iran, Iraq, Syria, and parts of Central Asia. The kingdom of Ptolemy I (died 283 BC) included Egypt and neighboring regions."[6]

History's Identification of the Fourth Kingdom

In order to identify the fourth beast (kingdom), which the prophet Daniel described as being diverse from the other three beasts before it, we must not only reexamine King Nebuchadnezzar's dream (Daniel 2) but also look to Daniel 7 and 8, which repeat and enlarge upon the king's dream.

King Nebuchadnezzar's Vision:
"His legs of iron, his feet part of iron and part of clay" (Daniel 2:33).

Daniel's Interpretation:
"And the fourth kingdom shall be strong as iron: forasmuch as iron breaketh in pieces and subdueth all things: and as iron that breaketh all these, shall it break in pieces and bruise" (Daniel 2:40).

Fourth Kingdom: Rome—a <u>strong and cohesive</u> kingdom (ca. AD 98-180)
"Historians disagree about the exact timing of Rome's golden age or High Empire, but the general consensus is that it stretched roughly over the reign of four emperors, beginning with Trajan, who ruled from AD 98 to 117 and was known as the *optimus princeps* (best ruler) by later generations of Romans."[7]

"In the second century CE, under Trajan, Hadrian, and the Antonines, the Roman Empire reached its greatest geographic extent and the height of its power. Rome's might was unchallenged in the Mediterranean world. . . . Within the empire's secure boundaries, the Pax Romana meant unprecedented prosperity for all who came under Roman rule."[8]

"If a man were called to fix the period in the history of the world, during which the condition of the human race was most happy and prosperous, he would, without hesitation, name that which elapsed from the death of Domitian to the accession of Commodus. The vast extent of the Roman empire was governed by absolute power, under the guidance of virtue and wisdom. The armies were restrained by the firm but gentle hand of four successive emperors, whose characters and authority commanded involuntary respect. The forms of the civil administration were carefully preserved by Nerva, Trajan, Hadrian, and the Antonines, who delighted in the image of liberty, and were pleased with considering themselves as the accountable ministers of the laws. Such princes deserved the honor of restoring the republic, had the Romans of their days been capable of enjoying a rational freedom."[9]

Daniel's Continued Interpretation:

"And whereas thou sawest the feet and toes, part of potter's clay, and part of iron, the [fourth] kingdom shall be divided; but there shall be in it of the strength of iron, forasmuch as thou sawest the iron mixed with miry clay" (Daniel 2:41).

Fourth Kingdom: Rome—a <u>divided</u> kingdom (AD 395)

"The Roman Empire first became divided under Diocletianus (284-305), who divided the empire into East and West territories in order to maintain efficient government control over the enormous empire. . . . The Empire was permanently divided in 395 upon the death of Theodosius who divided the empire between his two sons."[10]

"Diocletian [also known as Diocletianus] sought a formula which would preserve the unity of the Empire, maintain his own autocratic power, and provide an orderly succession of emperors without the intervention of the army. He divided the Empire into eastern and western portions and appointed a colleague to rule the West, while he governed the East and exercised a general control over both halves."[11]

"With his [Theodosius'] death in 395 the Roman Empire was permanently divided into Eastern and Western Empires. Whatever the devices employed thereafter to preserve the fiction of imperial unity, the Empire was clearly partitioned into two independent states by the end of the fourth century."[12]

Daniel's Continued Interpretation:

"And as the toes of the feet were part of iron, and part of clay, so the kingdom shall be partly strong, and partly broken" (Daniel 2:42).

Fourth Kingdom: Rome—a <u>partly strong and partly broken</u> kingdom (AD 476)

"In 476 barbarian mercenaries deposed the last Western Roman emperor, a boy whose name, Romulus Augustulus, by a strange irony recalled the founder of Rome and the founder of the Empire. In his place they elevated Odoacer, a fellow German. This episode marks the formal end of the Western Roman Empire. . . . With the disappearance of the Roman emperor of the West, the Eastern emperor claimed to be the source of authority, and his overlordship was recognized at least nominally by the new Germanic kings of the West who sought to gain from Constantinople acquiescence in their rule."[13]

"In 476, seventy-five years after the Goths had first entered Italy, the last Roman emperor resident in the West, the young and aptly named Romulus Augustulus (Romulus 'the little emperor'), was deposed and sent into retirement. The West was now ruled by independent Germanic kings. By contrast, the eastern Roman empire (which we often call the 'Byzantine empire') did not fall, despite pressure from the Goths, and later from the Huns. . . . Only in 1453 did the Byzantine empire finally disappear, when its capital and last bastion, Constantinople, fell to the Turkish army of Mehmed 'the Conqueror.'"[14]

The Fourth Kingdom: "A Little Horn"

Daniel 8 repeats and enlarges upon Daniel 7 with the vision of two other beasts, their horns, and one notable "little horn" that rises from the west and waxes exceedingly strong towards the other three corners of the earth.

Daniel's Vision:

"And as I was considering, behold, an he [male] goat came from the west on the face of the whole earth, and touched not the ground: and the goat had a notable horn between his eyes. . . . And I saw him [the he goat] come close unto the ram, and he was moved with choler against him, and smote the ram, and brake his two horns: and there was no power in the ram to stand before him, but he cast him down to the ground, and stamped upon him: and there was none that could deliver the ram out of his hand. Therefore the he goat waxed very great: and when he was strong, the great horn was broken; and for it came up four notable ones [horns] toward the four winds of heaven. And out of one of them came forth a little horn, which waxed exceeding great" (Daniel 8:5-9).

Gabriel's Interpretation:
"The ram which thou sawest having two horns are the kings of Media and Persia. And the rough goat is the king of Grecia [Greece]: and the great horn that is between his eyes is the first king [Alexander the Great]. Now that being broken, whereas four [horns] stood up for it, four kingdoms shall stand up out of the nation, but not in his [Alexander's] power. And in the latter time of their kingdom . . . a king of fierce countenance, and understanding dark sentences, shall stand up. And his power shall be mighty" (Daniel 8:20-24).

When comparing Daniel's two visions, it is evident that the ram and the goat in chapter 8 represent the same kingdoms as the bear and the leopard in chapter 7.

Daniel 8	Daniel 7
Ram with one horn higher than the other (verse 3)	Bear with one shoulder higher than the other (verse 5)
Goat with four horns (verse 8)	Leopard with four heads (verse 6)
Goat touches not the ground (verse 5)	Leopard with four wings (verse 6)

Furthermore, when comparing the fourth beast (kingdom) of Daniel 7 with the little horn power seen in Daniel 8, we see evidence to suggest that the two are one and the same entity.

Daniel's First Vision:
"After this I saw in the night visions, and behold a fourth beast, dreadful and terrible, and **strong exceedingly**; and it had great iron teeth: it devoured and brake in pieces, and stamped the residue with the feet of it: and it was diverse from all the beasts that were before it; and it had ten horns" (Daniel 7:7).

Daniel's Second Vision:
"And out of one of them [the four winds of heaven] came forth a little horn, **which waxed exceeding great**, toward the south, and toward the east, and toward the pleasant land [of Palestine]" (Daniel 8:9).

As for the strength of this little horn power, Daniel 8 tells us that it would be greater than all its predecessors.

Daniel 8:4: The ram "became **great**"
Daniel 8:8: The he goat "waxed **very great**"
Daniel 8:9: The little horn "waxed **exceeding great**"

This also concurs with King Nebuchadnezzar's dream of a great metallic image, in which the fourth kingdom (represented as having the physical properties of iron) was to be stronger than the previous three kingdoms represented by the softer metals of bronze, silver, and gold.

Fourth Kingdom: Rome—the "<u>little horn</u>" kingdom (168 BC)
History confirms what prophecy tells us in that Rome first flexed its military might against the divided Grecian empire to the east, soundly defeating the Macedonians at the Battle of Pydna (168 BC). Afterwards, it conquered the remaining Hellenistic monarchies of Macedonia (148 BC). Rome's rule and power eventually encompassed the territories of Syria (64 BC) and Palestine (63 BC) to the east and Egypt to the south (30 BC).

"Under the successors of Alexander, Syria was the Seleucidae, who reigned over Upper Asia. . . . When Syria became subject to the Romans, it formed the eastern frontier of their empire . . . and towards the south the confines of Egypt, and the Red Sea. Phoenicia and Palestine were sometimes annexed to, and sometimes separated from, the jurisdiction of Syria."[15]

"Whether it was these events that stirred the Romans into faster action against Macedonia or not is uncertain. The fact remains that the [Roman] consul of 168 [BC], Aemilius Paullus, marched north in

Greece with the immediate aim of confronting Perseus. Their armies met at Pydna in Pieria on the Thermaic Gulf. . . . The battle ended in a Roman bloodbath: 20,000 Macedonians were killed. Pydna marked the end of Macedonia as an independent kingdom: the first of the Hellenistic monarchies to be abolished."[16]

"In 148 B.C., Rome seized control of Macedonia and made it a Roman province."[17]

"Civil wars and attacks by outside forces weakened the power of the Seleucids, and in 64 B.C. the Roman general Pompey annexed Syria and made it a province of the Roman empire."[18]

"In 63 B.C., the Roman general Pompey seized Jerusalem."[19]

"With the death of Cleopatra in 30 B.C., the dynasty ended, and Egypt became a part of the Roman empire."[20]

To suggest that the pompous Seleucid (Syrian) king Antiochus IV Epiphanes was the little horn power that "waxed exceeding great," as Counter-Reformation preterists choose to believe, is to ignore the historical record, which shows Antiochus' kingdom to have been inferior in strength to both the Grecian Empire under Alexander the Great and the iron scepter of Rome during the time of Antiochus' rule (175-163 B.C.). Rome's superiority over Antiochus is clearly illustrated by the following incident:

"The 'day of Eleusis' lives in infamy. C. Popillius Laenas [a Roman consul] brusquely confronted the king of Syria [Antiochus IV] in that village on the outskirts of Alexandria and delivered the *senatus consultum.* . . . Humble acquiescence followed. Seleucid troops were removed from Egypt, and Popillius shortly thereafter cleared Antiochus' fleet out of Cyprus as well. The Sixth Syrian War was over, on Roman orders. The occasion has been taken as the keystone of Rome's farsighted and masterful diplomatic scheme and as the entrenchment of Roman control over the affairs of the East."[21]

The Lord God, whose divine power and sovereignty are over all the kings and kingdoms of this world, not only made known to the king of Babylon the future of his great and vast kingdom, but through His servant Daniel revealed to him the successive rise and fall of three other kingdoms to come. Given that God's omnipotence has been confirmed by history, we have the historical assurance that Daniel's final prediction (Daniel 2:44-45) shall surely come to pass: the kingdoms of this world shall pass away at the coming of God's kingdom (the fifth and final kingdom), which shall reign forever upon the earth.

For an overview and chart of Daniel's kingdom prophecies, see Appendix A.

Summary:

From a king's troubling dream to a prophet's frightening visions, the book of Daniel reveals to us God's foreknowledge as to the rise and fall of four worldly kingdoms. In Daniel 2, we see the vision of a great metallic image of a man being shattered by and replaced with a rock cut out of a mountain without hands. In Daniel 7, we see the imagery of four carnivorous beasts coming up out of a stormy sea. In Daniel 8, we see the fierce battle scene between a ram and a goat and their broken-off horns followed by the fierce countenance of a little horn power rising up in the west. In all of these visionary dreams and symbolic imagery, we see not only the rise and fall of four worldly kingdoms, but the fading glory of man's vanities, strife, and vexation of spirit in comparison with God's everlasting glory and never-ending kingdom of peace to come.

> *"I saw in the night visions, and, behold, one like the Son of man came with the clouds of heaven, and came to the Ancient of days, and they brought him near before him. And there was given him dominion, and glory, and a kingdom, that all people, nations, and languages, should serve him: his dominion is an everlasting dominion, which shall not pass away, and his kingdom that which shall not be destroyed." Daniel 7:13-14*

Notes:

1. Austen Henry Layard, *Discoveries Among the Ruins of Nineveh and Babylon* (New York: George P. Putnam & Co., 1853), 453-454

2. J. B. Bury, S. A. Cook, F. E. Adcock, eds., *The Cambridge Ancient History*, vol. 4, "The Persian Empire and the West" (London: Cambridge Univ. Press, 1926), 2

3. Ibid., 8

4. Jean-Pierre Isbouts, *The Biblical World: An Illustrated Atlas* (USA, National Geographic Society, 2007), 245

5. John Boardman, Jasper Griffin, Oswyn Murray, eds., *The Oxford Illustrated History of Greece and the Hellenistic World* (Oxford, England: Oxford Univ. Press, 1988), 311

6. Edward Weller, *Kingdoms of the Successors of Alexander: After the Battle of Ipsus, B.C. 301* (London: Edward Weller, between 1800 and 1899). Map. https://www.wdl.org/en/item/11739/

7. Amy Chua, *Day of Empire* (New York: Anchor Books, 2007), 37

8. Fred Kleiner, *Gardner's Art Through the Ages: A Global History*, 13th ed. (Boston, MA: Thomson Wadsworth, 2009), 263

9. H. H. Milman, ed., *The History of the Decline and Fall of the Roman Empire by Edward Gibbon*, vol. 1 (London: John Murray, 1839), 136

10. William L. Langer, ed., *An Encyclopedia of World History*, 4th ed. (Boston, MA: Houghton Mifflin Co., 1968), 131-134

11. Solomon Katz, *The Decline of Rome and the Rise of Mediaeval Europe* (Ithaca, NY: Cornell Univ. Press, 1955), 44

12. Ibid., 90

13. Ibid., 93

14. Bryan Ward-Perkins, *The Fall of Rome and the End of Civilization* (USA: Oxford Univ. Press, 2005), 2

15. Milman, ed., *The History of the Decline and Fall of the Roman Empire by Edward Gibbon*, vol. 1, 39

16. Peter Green, *The Hellenistic Age: A Short History* (USA: Modern Library, 2007), 93

17. Carroll Moulton, ed., *Ancient Greece and Rome: An Encyclopedia for Students*, vol. 2 (New York: Holiday House, 1998), 126

18. Ibid., vol. 4, 73

19. Ibid., vol. 2, 170

20. Ibid., vol. 3, 164

21. Erich S. Gruen, *The Hellenistic World and the Coming of Rome*, vols. 1-2 (Berkeley, CA: Univ. of California Press, 1984), 658-659

Chapter Eight

The Little Horn's Image

*"I considered the [ten] horns, and, behold, there came up
among them another little horn, before whom there were
three of the first [ten] horns plucked up by the roots: and,
behold, in this horn were eyes like the eyes of man, and a
mouth speaking great things." Daniel 7:8*

In addition to the little horn (the Roman Empire) that rose to
power and waxed exceedingly great (Daniel 8:9), Bible prophecy tells
us of another little horn power that would later rise to power within
the Roman Empire among ten kings (kingdoms). History shows us that
after the Roman Empire was divided in 395 AD, its western division
became subdivided among the invading Germanic tribes.

As to the identity of the ten Germanic kings or kingdoms of which
Bible prophecy speaks, historians and theologians are in disagree-
ment. Yet most, if not all, agree that the Roman Catholic Church rose
to power among the Germanic kingdoms to become a domineering
political-religious power throughout all of western medieval Europe.
The question, then, to be answered is: Does the Roman Catholic
Church (Roman papacy) fulfill Bible prophecy as being the little horn
power that came up among ten horns (kingdoms)?

Daniel's Vision:
"I considered the [ten] horns, and, behold, there came up among
them another little horn, before whom there were three of the first [ten]

horns plucked up by the roots: and, behold, in this horn were eyes like the eyes of man, and a mouth speaking great things" (Daniel 7:8).

Gabriel's Interpretation:
"And the ten horns out of this [fourth] kingdom are ten kings that shall arise: and another shall arise after them; and he shall be diverse from the first, and he shall subdue three kings. And he shall speak great words against the most High [God], and shall wear out the saints of the most High, and think to change times and laws: and they shall be given into his hand until a time and times and the dividing of time" (Daniel 7:24-25).

Daniel 7 provides us with eight prophetic-historical markers for identifying the little horn power that rose up in Rome's place.

1) Arises out of the fourth kingdom, Rome (verses 7, 20)
"And if a man consider[s] the original of this great ecclesiastical dominion, he will easily perceive that the papacy is no other than the ghost of the deceased Roman Empire, sitting crowned upon its grave thereof: for so did the papacy start up on a sudden out of the ruins of that heathen power."[1]

"This decaying Empire, after a futile contest with Christianity, was to become its servant. The mighty Catholic Church was little more than the Roman Empire baptized. Rome was transformed as well as converted. The very capital of the old Empire became the capital of the Christian Empire."[2]

"When the [Roman] Empire passed away, the [Roman] church succeeded and superseded it. Upon the foundation of the triumphant Christian religion the new world of the Middle Ages was slowly erected."[3]

2) Comes up among ten western kingdoms (verses 8, 20)
"The fourth to the seventh centuries mark the decline of the ancient world and the birth of the mediaeval. . . . During these centuries the western half of the Empire was lost to the Germanic invaders, who succeeded in establishing kingdoms of their own on its soil."[4]

The Germanic tribes that existed along the northern border of the Western Empire (ca. AD 400) included the Picts, Jutes, Angles, Saxons, Franks, Burgundians, Alemanni, Sueves, Vandals, and Goths. By AD 500, these warring tribes had been either absorbed, split apart, or enlarged in their conquests throughout the declining Western Empire. For this reason alone, historians and theologians alike have a difficult time in deciding which among them and their offshoots make up the ten kings of Daniel's prophecy. But one thing is for sure: their former kingdoms stand as a testament to what is still today a divided Europe as Daniel had predicted: "And as the toes of the feet were part of iron and part of clay, so the kingdom shall be partly strong, and partly broken. . . . They shall mingle themselves with the seed of men: but they shall not cleave one to another, even as iron is not mixed with clay" (Daniel 2:42-43).

3) More stout than the other ten kingdoms (verse 20)

"In the vacuum created by the transfer and eventually by the fall of the imperial government in the West, the popes became more active in the administration and even in the defense of the city [Rome] and achieved a sovereignty which extended from ecclesiastical to civil affairs [a religious-political power]."[5]

"Under the Roman Empire the popes had no temporal power. But when the Roman Empire had disintegrated and its place had been taken by a number of rude barbarous kingdoms, the Roman Catholic Church not only became independent of the states in religious affairs but dominated secular affairs as well."[6]

"Long ages ago when Rome through neglect of the Western emperors was left to the mercy of the barbarous hordes, the Romans turned to one figure for aid and protection, and asked him to rule them; and thus in this simple manner, the best title of all to kingly right, commenced the temporal sovereignty of the popes. And meekly stepping to the throne of Caesar, the vicar of Christ took up the scepter to which the emperors and kings of Europe were to bow in reverence through so many ages."[7]

4) Arises after three kingdoms have been subdued (verses 8, 20, 24)

Not long after Emperor Justinian's decree making the bishop of Rome the head of all the churches (AD 533), the Eastern Roman Empire under Justinian's warring generals subdued three Arian kingdoms. Located in the Empire's three westernmost provinces, these kingdoms were the Vandals in North Africa, the Ostrogoths in Italy, and the Visigoths in Spain.

AD 533-4: The Vandals were uprooted from Africa

"Vandal power slowly declined after 477 as a result of internal and external pressures. Their rule in North Africa ended in 533 when Byzantine forces sent by Emperor Justinian I easily defeated the Vandal army. Within a short time, all traces of Vandal occupation had disappeared."[8]

"The powerful Vandal kingdom in North Africa did not last long. In A.D. 533 the emperor Justinian sent an army—under the command of his great general, Belisarius—against the Vandals. The Romans quickly crushed them and destroyed their kingdom."[9]

AD 553: The Ostrogoths were uprooted from Italy

"Teias, Totila's successor and the last Ostrogothic King of Italy, sought the assistance of the Franks. Before he could be able to obtain this aid, he was defeated and killed at Cumae in A.D. 553. . . . The defeat and death of Teias put an end to the Ostrogothic kingdom in Italy, which had existed sixty years (A.D. 493-553). Italy then became a province of the Eastern Roman Empire, the Emperor Justinian erecting the conquered country into the Exarchate of Ravenna."[10]

AD 555: The Visigoths were uprooted from southern Spain

"Turning to Spain, the emperor apparently sent reinforcements that landed at Cartagena late in 554. By the next March their westward advance to meet their allies seems to have frightened the loyalist Visigoths into killing King Agila and proclaiming his rival Athanagild. After becoming king, Athanagild tried to thank and dismiss Justinian's soldiers. However, no doubt following the emperor's orders, they refused to leave or submit to Athanagild, and they were joined by the

Romans of Cordova who had rebelled against Agila in the first place. Thus the Visigoths lost southern Spain to a combination of their former Roman subjects and the imperial troops, who held about a fifth of the peninsula."[11]

"Militarily, the eastern and northern frontiers were Justinian's chief concerns. . . . Nevertheless, in the 530s the emperor took advantage of political instability in the Vandal kingdom of North Africa and the Ostrogothic regime in Italy to attempt to restore direct Roman rule over these territories. . . . North Africa fell in 533-4 and Italy was reduced between 535 and 553. In the early 550s, Justinian's armies were even able to establish a foothold in southern Spain. These victories did much to restore the empire to a position of political, ideological, and military dominance in the central and western Mediterranean."[12]

"A good deal of the former Roman territory still remained to be recovered, but Italy, the greater part of North Africa, and part of Spain, with the Mediterranean islands, had been seized from the Germans and brought under the scepter of the Roman Emperor of Constantinople. The Mediterranean was once more a Roman lake."[13]

To suggest that the Heruli kingdom was one of the three uprooted horns (kingdoms), as some scholars believe, is to ignore the historical record, which indicates that the Heruli kingdom had already been destroyed several decades earlier. The Heruli were defeated by the Ostrogoths, who in turn were defeated by the Eastern Roman Empire.

"By the murder of Odoacer [AD 493] the Kingdom of the Heruli in Italy came to an end, and Theodoric the Ostrogoth thus became sole King of Italy, establishing his capital at Ravenna."[14]

5) Reigns for 1260 years (verse 25)
The little horn's time of dominion over God's saints is measured here as "a time and times and the dividing of time" and in Daniel 12:7 as "a time, times, and an half." The word for "time" in this verse means "year," so "time" = 1 year, "times" = 2 years, and "half a time" = ½ year, for a sum of 3½ years. By following the principle of a prophetic day

equaling a literal year (see prophetic principle 4 in Chapter 4), we can see that 3½ years x 360 days/year (lunar calendar) = **1260 prophetic days or 1260 literal years.**

In the book of Revelation, which repeats and expands upon Daniel's timeline prophecies, we find this same language being used in Revelation 12:14: "a time, and times, and half a time." It is further interpreted in Revelation 12:6 to mean "a thousand two hundred and threescore days" (1260 days).

History confirms Daniel's prophetic timelines, revealing the extent of the Roman papacy's temporal reign (1260 years), which began in AD 610 and ended in 1870. History also shows that the papacy's rise to power began 30 years earlier in AD 580. Daniel 12:11 refers to this entire period of 1290 days (years).

For an overview and the historical dates of Daniel's timeline prophecies, see Appendix B.

AD 580-610: The Roman papacy's rise to temporal power

Ancient Rome's glory and power steadily declined with the systematic dismantling and decay of its civil government. In AD 330, Emperor Constantine relocated the executive branch of the Roman Empire to his new home and city of Constantinople. In AD 541, Emperor Justinian abolished the second branch of government, the Consulate. By AD 580, the third and remnant branch of government, the Senate, had all but faded from existence, and along with it any remaining stronghold of the traditional Roman pagan religion.

In the absence of Rome's civil authority, the Church of Rome in the short time span of thirty years (AD 580-610) rose up to become a religious-political power in the city of Rome and eventually the western half of the ancient Roman empire.

AD 580: The Roman Senate is all but extinct.

"These writers [Hegal, Giesebrecht, Gregorovius] believe that after the middle of the 6th century the senate had a merely nominal existence. According to Gregorovius its last appearance was in the year 579 [580].[15] After that date it is mentioned in no documents, and the chroniclers are either equally silent or merely allude to its decay and extinction."[16]

"Nominally the city [Rome] came under the jurisdiction of the Byzantine exarchy at Ravenna, attested by 584, but in practice the popes took over more and more of the secular administration and authority, finding suitable powerful leaders in Pelagius and Gregory the Great. The Roman Senate is last mentioned in 580; Rome was on the way to becoming a papal state—and the next 1,400 years of its history are another story."[17]

"Gregory, in one of his homilies, exclaims, 'Where is the Senate? Where are the People? . . . All the glory of the earthly dignity has expired from the city. All her greatness has vanished. . . . Because there is no Senate, the People perished.'"[18]

AD 580: The city of Rome is left to fend for herself.

"The Lombards began encroaching on Italian territories—an invasion which would have significant consequences for the popes, although the Lombards never managed to conquer Rome."[19]

"Pelagius II stressed the primacy [the authority of the pope over the church] when seeking help for beleaguered Rome from Bishop Aunacharius [also known as Aunarius] of Auxerre: 'It would have been more seemly if you other limbs of the Catholic church, bound together in the one body under the direction of one head, had hurried with all your strength to aid our peace and our contentment in the unity of the Holy Spirit.'"[20]

"In Oct. 580, therefore, [Pope] Pelagius appealed to Aunarius, bishop of Auxerre; as neighbours sharing the orthodox faith, he pleaded, Providence had singled out the Franks to be Rome's and Italy's Protectors. His appeal fell on deaf ears, and four years later he had to write to Gregory in Constantinople describing Italy's plight and urging him to bestir the emperor."[21]

"His [Pelagius II's] appeals to Constantinople were fruitless as the emperor had problems of his own in fending off Persian attacks, and it was not until 585 that Constantinople reached an accommodative truce with the Lombard leaders."[22]

AD 590-604: Pope Gregory solidifies the church's temporal rule.
"Pope Gregory I proved himself not only one of the most saintly men who had held this high office, but also an administrator, statesman and diplomat of exceptional gifts, the creator of the medieval papacy."[23]

"The power of the papacy was greatly strengthened, and, indeed, the foundations of the mediaeval papacy were established by a series of able leaders . . . and finally by Pope Gregory the Great (590-604), who brought the whole orthodox Christian world in close connection with the See of Peter."[24]

"Pope Gregory died in 604. He left the papacy efficiently adminis-tered, fully capable of managing its own affairs as well as those of the temporal government, rich enough not only to maintain its buildings and to see to the wants of the clergy, but also to care for the poor, to pay officials to govern the State and for troops to defend it, and to represent Rome in her uneasy relations with Byzantium, still theoretically her overlord."[25]

AD 607: Papal supremacy is affirmed.
"A skillful diplomat, he [Boniface III] established friendly relations with [King] Phocas, and when he became pope [in AD 607] obtained from him a formal declaration that Rome, the see of St. Peter, was head of all the churches. Emperor Justinian (527-65) had issued a similar pronouncement, but this time it put a stop, for the moment at any rate, to the claim of bishops of Constantinople, exasperating to Pelagius II and Gregory I, to the title 'ecumenical patriarch.' The occasion was marked by the erection in Rome of a gilded statue of the tyrannical Phocas with an adulatory inscription."[26]

"Boniface was a more successful diplomat than Sabinian . . . and he won the support of the imperial court for the papacy and obtained from Phocas a decree repeating the Novella (Corpus euris civilis, Novellae 131.2.14) of Justinian, whereby the Roman pontiff was rec-ognized as head of all churches. This pronouncement contradicted the title 'ecumenical patriarch' then recently assumed by the Patriarch of Constantinople, John IV the Faster."[27]

AD 609/610: The pagan Pantheon is Christianized.

The Pantheon was ancient Rome's most holy pagan temple, dedicated to the worship of all the Roman gods. There is no precise date in history as to when the temple building was refurbished as a Christian church, but most historians place Pope Boniface IV's dedication in May 609 or 610. The abandoned pagan temple and its relics were rededicated to the Virgin Mary and all the martyred saints.

"The most remarkable event of his [Boniface's] pontificate was the consecration of the Basilica Sancta Maria ad Martyres on the site of the Pantheon. The Emperor Phocas had acceded to the pope's request for the conversion of the ancient pagan monument into a Christian church, and Boniface translated there a number of relics from the catacombs."[28]

"Boniface obtained leave from the Emperor Phocas to convert the Pantheon into a Christian Church, and on 13 May, 609 (?) the temple erected by Agrippa to Jupiter the Avenger, to Venus, and to Mars was consecrated by the pope to the Virgin Mary and all the Martyrs. . . . It was the first instance at Rome of the transformation of a pagan temple into a place of Christian worship."[29]

AD 610: The beginning of the Roman papacy's temporal power

The reign of the new Eastern emperor Heraclius (AD 610-41) marks the point in history when the Roman papacy's power in the West went unchecked by what little power remained from the ancient Roman Empire, now centered in the Eastern (Byzantine) Empire. The Roman papacy's system of government (a theocracy) quickly did away with many of the long-standing religious and civil liberties enacted by the Republic of Rome, which had been founded in 510/509 BC.

"The Empire lay in ruins when the government was taken over by Heraclius (610-41). . . . The country was economically and financially exhausted and the worn-out administrative machinery had come to a standstill. Military organization, based on mercenary recruitment, no longer functioned, for there was no money, nor were the old sources of man-power any longer available. The vital central provinces of the Empire were overrun by the enemy: Slavs and Avars were settling in

the Balkans and the Persians were entrenching themselves in the heart
of Asia Minor. Only internal regeneration could save the Empire from
destruction."[30]

"Never had any of his [Heraclius's] predecessors inherited so des-
perate a situation. To the west, the Avars and the Slavs had overrun
the Balkans, their raiding parties regularly approaching the very gates
of Constantinople; to the east the Persian watch-fires at Chalcedon,
immediately across the Bosphorus, were clearly visible from the win-
dows of the imperial palace. . . . But though the centre of the Empire
might remain secure, the extremities were fast falling away."[31]

AD 1870: The end of the Roman papacy's temporal power

During the 1260 day-year prophetic time period (AD 610-1870),
the Roman Catholic Church not only built upon the foundations laid
by Pope Gregory I, "The Father of Christian Worship," but audaciously
declared itself to be the sole gatekeeper of man's access to God and
eternal salvation. It became the dominant and authoritative state religion of medieval Europe, and its ecclesiastical and political dictates
were mandated as law. Anyone who dared to oppose its authority or
rule was labeled a heretic against Christianity and rooted out. During
the protracted time period of the Inquisitions (1231-1834), the Cru-
sades (1095-1492), and the Protestant Reformation (1517-1648), many
innocent souls were persecuted, exiled, imprisoned, tortured, and even
killed.

It is most interesting to note that in the same year that the Roman
papacy declared itself to be infallible (1870), its temporal reign came
to a prophetic and literal end with the fall of papal Rome to the king
of Italy—Victor Emmanuel II, "Father of the Fatherland." The Roman
pontiff, now a king without a kingdom, confined himself as a prisoner
behind the walls of the Vatican.

"In 1860 the Papal States were annexed to the newly created kingdom of Italy leaving only Rome itself to the pope. In 1870 the French
were obligated to retire from Rome to take part in the Franco-Prus-
sian War. Soon after, soldiers led by Giuseppe Garibaldi, a republican
patriot, occupied the city and the pope had to conclude an agreement

with him. This left the Vatican independent of the new secular gov-ernment, but its independence was short-lived. After a plebiscite on 1 October 1870, Rome was annexed by the new kingdom of Italy and became its capital."[32]

"Almost simultaneously in 1870 Vatican Council I established the pope permanently at the pinnacle of spiritual power, and an invading Italian army ended the papal temporal power."[33]

"At the present time systematic Papal persecution has been wholly discontinued. Ever since the year 1870, the Pope and Curia have been debarred the exercise of temporal power, and civil governments have recognised, on the whole, that impartial protection of the true interests of the people better safeguards the State than an attempt to exercise by persecution uniformity in religious belief and observance."[34]

Some scholars put AD 1798, when the French army took the pope captive, as the prophetic end date for the papacy's temporal reign as indicated by the 1260 day-year prophecy. However, history clearly shows us that much of the papacy's civil authority was reinstated by Napoleon in 1801 (Concordat of 1801) and that it wasn't until 1870 that it was permanently removed, thus historically and prophetically ending the papacy's temporal reign in Europe.

6) Speaks great (blasphemous) words (verse 25)

Revelation 13:5 repeats and expands upon Daniel 7:25: "And there was given unto him a mouth speaking great things and blasphemies." The Bible's definition of blasphemy includes the sacrilegious claim of authority to forgive sins (Luke 5:21) as well as the impious claim of being man's rightful intercessor, both of which are the prerogatives of the Lord alone (John 10:33). In contrast to the Bible's teachings, the following bold statements have been made by the Roman Catholic Church and its popes (see table on next page):

What the Roman Papacy Says . . .	**What God's Word Says . . .**
"We declare, we proclaim, we define that it is absolutely necessary for salvation that every human creature be subject to the Roman Pontiff."—Pope Boniface VIII, *Unam Sanctam*, November 18, 1302 [35]	"In Him [Jesus] we have redemption through His [Jesus'] blood, the forgiveness of our trespasses, according to the riches of His [Jesus'] grace, which He [Jesus] lavished upon us" (Ephesians 1:7-8, NASB).
"This is Our last lesson to you: receive it, engrave it in your minds, all of you: by God's commandment salvation is to be found nowhere but in the Church; the strong and effective instrument of salvation is none other than the Roman Pontificate."—Pope Leo XIII, Allocution for the 25th anniversary of his election, February 20, 1903 [36]	"And there is salvation in no one else [but Jesus]; for there is no other name under heaven that has been given among men by which we must be saved" (Acts 4:12, NASB).
"He [the Vicar of Christ] is the intermediary between God and man: beneath God, above man: less than God, more than man: he judges all, and is judged by none."—sermon of Pope Innocent III, preached at his own consecration, AD 1198 [37]	"Jesus said . . . , 'I am the way, and the truth, and the life; no one comes to the Father, but through me'" (John 14:6, NASB). "Hence, also, He [Jesus] is able to save forever those who draw near to God through Him, since He always lives to make intercession for them" (Hebrews 7:25, NASB).
"Sins committed before Baptism are forgiven by Baptism. Sins committed after Baptism are forgiven in the Sacrament of Penance and Reconciliation, also called the Sacrament of Forgiveness, Confession and Conversion."[38]	"And if anyone sins, we have an Advocate with the Father, Jesus Christ the righteous; and He himself is the propitiation for our sins; and not for ours only, but also for those of the whole world" (1 John 2:1-2, NASB).
"On Easter night the Risen Christ imparted to his Apostles his own power to forgive sins. . . . By the Sacrament of Holy Orders, bishops and priests continue this ministry to forgive sins. . . . In this Sacrament, the priest acts in the person of Christ, the Head of the Church, to reconcile the sinner to both God and the Church."[39]	"Since then we have a great high priest who has passed through the heavens, Jesus the Son of God, let us hold fast our confession. . . . Let us therefore draw near with confidence to the throne of grace, that we may receive mercy and may find grace to help in time of need" (Hebrews 4:14-16, NASB).

When Jesus passed from this world into heaven, He became our great high priest and only intercessor before God. Therefore, let us draw near to Him with a sincere heart and in faith lay all our burdens and sins at His feet. Because He has given Himself as the perfect sacrifice for our sins, once and for all, we may have full confidence in the promise of His Word: "If we confess our sins, he is faithful and just to forgive us our sins, and to cleanse us from all unrighteousness" (1 John 1:9).

7) Makes war with and wears out the saints of God (verses 21, 25)

"That the Church of Rome has shed more innocent blood than any other institution that has ever existed among mankind, will be questioned by no Protestant who has a competent knowledge of history. . . . It is impossible to form a complete conception of the multitude of her victims, and it is quite certain that no powers of imagination can adequately realize their sufferings."[40]

"The simple-minded and humble student of God's word . . . finds Holy Scripture and the records of even Roman historians uniting in the fullest harmony to establish the fact, that from the commencement of the mystic 1260 years, to its close, there was existing in Europe a Great Spiritual Tyranny;—and that by this Tyranny 'the Saints,' [anti-papalists] whether Paulicians, Cathari, Vaudois [Waldensians], Albigeois, or Lollards, — were uniformly 'warred against;' and until the close of the allotted period were 'worn out,' — 'prevailed against,' — and 'slain.'"[41]

"Another painful chapter of history to which the sons and daughters of the church must return with a spirit of repentance is that of the acquiescence given, especially in certain centuries, to intolerance and even to use of violence in the service of truth."[42]

8) Thinks to change times and laws (verse 25)

"The division and numbering of the [Ten] Commandments have varied in the course of history. The present catechism follows the division of the Commandments established by St. Augustine, which has become traditional in the [Roman] Catholic Church."[43]

The Traditional Catechetical Commandments:

1) I am the LORD your God: you shall not have strange Gods before me.
2) You shall not take the name of the LORD your God in vain.
3) Remember to keep holy the LORD'S Day (Sunday).
4) Honor your father and your mother.
5) You shall not kill.
6) You shall not commit adultery.
7) You shall not steal.
8) You shall not bear false witness against your neighbor.
9) You shall not covet your neighbor's wife.
10) You shall not covet your neighbor's goods.[44]

The catechetical formula removes from God's Law, the Holy Decalogue, any mention of the second commandment (no making of graven images), shortens and revises the fourth commandment (the Sabbath day), and subdivides the tenth commandment into two parts, thus revising God's Law.

Furthermore, with the shortening of God's fourth commandment, most Christians today have little or no understanding of the historical change in the day of worship. Under the Roman emperor Constantine, the Edict of Milan (AD 313) was enacted, which legalized Christianity. Constantine also endorsed Sunday as a day of rest and worship for all Roman citizens—a day that was celebrated and honored by the then state-subsidized Roman Church. Today most Christians unknowingly pay homage to Sunday, a day sanctified not by Scripture but by the sacred tradition of the Roman Catholic Church.

"CHRISTIANS shall not judaize by resting on the Sabbath [Saturday], but must work on that day, rather honouring the Lord's day [Sunday]; and, if they can, resting then as Christians. But if any shall be found to be judaizers, let them be anathema [shut out] from Christ."[45]

"But the Church of God [Roman Catholic Church] has in her wisdom ordained that the celebration of the Sabbath day [Saturday] should be transferred to 'the Lord's day' [Sunday]."[46]

As a mark of its authority and infallibility,[47] the little horn not only thought to change God's immutable Sabbath day from Saturday to Sunday and to label it the Lord's Day, but, as history shows, it also intended to change "times" or God's "appointed times." In response to the Protestants' claims that the prophetic books of Daniel and Revelation pointed to the papal system as being spiritually corrupt and having the character of antichrist, the Roman papacy soon brought forward in the Counter-Reformation (sometimes called the Catholic Reformation) two distinctly different methodologies for studying Bible prophecy. Together these two interpretative methods, preterism and futurism,[48] have successfully divided Christian thinking as well as removed the spotlight from the "appointed times" that point to the rise and fall and rise again of the little horn antichrist power.

Rising up in the place of ancient Rome, the Roman papacy (little horn kingdom) soon began to audaciously see itself as both priest and king. Because it claimed the prerogatives of God, including the keys of heaven and hell, the majority of medieval Christendom, including the royalty of Europe, submitted to its demands and dictates for fear of eternal damnation. Magnifying the pope as the Vicar of Christ on earth, the Roman Catholic Church through its priesthood not only sought to replace Jesus Christ's ministry in the heavenly sanctuary as the High Priest of our confession but in the daily mass crucified Christ afresh, thus making void His perfect sacrifice for sin, which was once and for all (Hebrews 10:10-12).

The Dark Ages ensued until light bearers such as John Wycliffe, John Huss, Jerome, Martin Luther, John Calvin, and other brave reformers began to steadily uncover the hidden truths of God's Word. During the time of the Protestant Reformation, many gave up their home, family ties, and life itself—all for the cause of freedom found in Jesus Christ as their Lord and Savior. As a countermeasure to the Protestant Reformation, the Roman papacy brought forward fear, confusion, and hostility towards anyone who refused to adhere to its dogmas and rule.

Sir Isaac Newton wrote:

> The little horn is a little kingdom. . . . But it was a kingdom of a different kind from the other ten kingdoms,

having a life or soul peculiar to itself, with eyes and a mouth. By its eyes it was a Seer; and by its mouth speaking great things, and changing times and laws, it was a Prophet as well as a King. And such a Seer, a Prophet and a King, is the Church of Rome. A Seer, is a Bishop in the literal sense of the word; and this Church claims the universal Bishoprick. With his mouth he gives laws to kings and nations as an Oracle; and pretends to Infallibility, and that his dictates are binding to the whole world; which is to be a Prophet in the highest degree."[49]

In AD 1798, France struck a blow to the Roman papacy by taking its pontiff hostage and temporarily removing its governing authority over the Papal States. In AD 1870, 1260 years after it began, the papacy's temporal reign finally came to an end when the city of Rome and the remaining Papal States were surrendered to the king of Italy.[50] As for the pontiff himself, he became a self-made prisoner behind the walls of the Vatican.

Summary:

Prophecy in the light of history clearly shows the ancient Roman Empire to be the dreadful and terrible fourth beast and persecuting power of Daniel's visions. As Daniel correctly predicted, the Roman Empire became divided, and its western half broke up into pieces, which then opened the way for a little horn power to rise up in ancient Rome's place. The Roman papacy historically fulfills Daniel's little horn prophecy, having risen up in ancient Rome's place to eventually rule over the ecclesiastical and secular affairs of western medieval Europe. Today the Roman papacy or "Holy See" is marveled at as being an independent and sovereign nation-state whose seat of government, Vatican City,[51] still resides in the ancient-modern city of Rome.

> "And another [little horn] shall rise. . . . And he shall shall speak great words against the most High, . . . and think to change times and laws: and they [the saints of the most High] shall be given into his hand until a time and times and the dividing of time." Daniel 7:24-25

Notes:

1. Thomas Hobbes, *Leviathan*, 4th ed. (London: George Routledge and Sons, Ltd., 1894), 313

http://www.ForgottenBooks.com

2. Alexander Clarence Flick, *The Rise of the Mediaeval Church* (New York: Burt Franklin, 1909), 149-150

3. Solomon Katz, *The Decline of Rome and the Rise of Mediaeval Europe* (Ithaca, NY: Cornell Univ. Press, 1955), 69

4. Ibid., 85

5. Ibid., 126

6. Carl Conrad Eckhardt, *The Papacy and World-Affairs as Reflected in the Secularization of Politics* (Chicago, IL: The Univ. of Chicago Press, 1937), 1

7. James P. Conry, "Two Romes," *American Catholic Quarterly Review*, vol. 36, April 1911, no. 142, 194

https://archive.org/details/AmeriCatholicQRevV36/page/n207

8. William C. Jordan, ed., *The Middle Ages: An Encyclopedia for Students*, vol. 4 (New York: Charles Scribner's Sons, 1996), 151

9. Carroll Moulton, ed., *Ancient Greece and Rome: An Encyclopedia for Students*, vol. 4 (New York, Holiday House, 1998), 113

10. John Herbert Clifford, ed., *The Standard History of the World by Great Historians*, vol. 3 (New York: The Univ. Society Inc., 1907), 1537-1538

11. Warren Treadgold, *A History of the Byzantine State and Society* (Stanford, CA: Stanford Univ. Press, 1997), 211

12. Cyril Mango, ed., *The Oxford History of Byzantium* (New York: Oxford Univ. Press, 2002), 46

13. George Ostrogorsky, *History of the Byzantine State* (New Brunswick, NJ: Rutgers Univ. Press, 1969), 71

14. Israel Smith Clare, *Library of Universal History and Popular Science*, vol. 5 (New York: The Bancroft Society, 1910), 1534

15. The Roman year was split over two modern years. AUC or "*Ab urbe condita*" is Latin for "from the founding of the City [Rome]." Year 1 AUC (754/753 BC) is traditionally set as the founding year of the City. The Roman Senate, which came into existence with the Republic of Rome in 245 AUC or 510/509 BC, ended in 1332 AUC or AD 579/580.

https://en.wikipedia.org/wiki/List_of_Roman_consuls#Chronology

16. Hugh Chisholm, ed., *The Encyclopedia Britannica*, 11th ed., vol. 23 (New York, The Encyclopedia Britannica Co., 1911), 663

17. Amanda Claridge, *Rome: An Oxford Archaeological Guide* (New York: Oxford Univ. Press, 2010), 32

18. F. Homes Dudden, *Gregory the Great: His Place in History and Thought*, vol. 1 (London: Longmans, Green, and Co., 1905), 185

19. P. G. Maxwell-Stuart, *Chronicle of the Popes* (London: Thames & Hudson, 1997), 47

20. Jeffery Richards, *Consul of God: The Life and Times of Gregory the Great* (London: Routledge & Kegan Paul, 1980), 63

21. J. N. D. Kelly, *The Oxford Dictionary of Popes* (Oxford: Oxford Univ. Press, 1986), 65

22. Maxwell-Stuart, *Chronicle of the Popes*, 47

23. Christopher Hibbert, *Rome: The Biography of a City* (London: Viking, 1985), 75

24. Katz, *The Decline of Rome and the Rise of Mediaeval Europe*, 126

25. Ibid., 78

26. Kelly, *The Oxford Dictionary of Popes*, 68

27. The Catholic University of America, *New Catholic Encyclopedia*, 2nd ed., vol. 2 (Farmington Hills, MI: Thomson/Gale, 2003), 499

28. Ibid.

29. Oestereich, Thomas. "Pope St. Boniface IV." *The Catholic Encyclopedia,* vol. 2 (New York: Robert Appleton Company, 1907), 661
http://www.newadvent.org/cathen/02660c.htm

30. George Ostrogorsky, *History of the Byzantine State*, 92

31. John Julius Norwich, *Byzantium: The Early Centuries* (London: Viking, 1988), 284

32. Maxwell-Stuart, *Chronicle of the Popes*, 218

33. The Catholic University of America, *New Catholic Encyclopedia,* 2nd ed., vol. 10 (Farmington Hills, MI: Thomson/Gale, 2003), 848

34. Charles H. H. Wright and Charles Neil, eds., *A Protestant Dictionary: Containing Articles on the History, Doctrines, and Practices of the Christian Church* (London: Ballantyne, Hanson & Co., 1904), 512

35. Paul Halsall, ed., "Medieval Sourcebook: Boniface VIII, Unam Sanctam, 1302" Internet History Sourcebooks Project. November 23, 1996
https://sourcebooks.fordham.edu/source/b8-unam.asp

36. Mother E'O Gorman, trans., *Papal Teachings: The Church* (Boston, MA: The Daughters of St. Paul, 1980), 353
http://thecatholicarchive.com/wp-content/uploads/2014/07/281.pdf

37. C. H. C. Pirie-Gordon, *Innocent the Great* (London: Longmans, Green, and Co., 1907), 226

38. United States Conference of Catholic Bishops, *United States Catholic Catechism for Adults* (Washington, D.C.: USCCB Publishing, 2006), 245

39. Ibid., 236

40. W. E. H. Leecky, *History of the Rise and Influence of the Spirit of Rationalism in Europe*, 2nd ed., vol. 2 (London: Longmans, Green, and Co., 1865), 35

41. Charlotte Elizabeth, *War With the Saints; or Persecutions of the Vaudois Under Pope Innocent III* (New York: M. W. Dodd, 1848), 301

42. Pope John Paul II, "*Terito Millennio Adveniente*" (Latin for "*As the third millennium approaches*"), apostolic letter, November 10, 1994

43. United States Catholic Conference, *Catechism of the Catholic Church*, 2nd ed. (Washington, D.C.: USCCB Publishing, 2007), 496-497

44. Ibid.

45. Council of Laodicea, Canon 29 (ca. AD 363-364) http://www.newadvent.org/fathers/3806.htm

46. J. Donovan, trans., *Catechism of the Council of Trent: Translated into English* (Dublin, Ireland: Richard Coyne, 1829), 379

47. The doctrine of papal infallibility was formally defined in AD 1870 by the First Vatican Council.

48. See Chapter 4 for an explanation of these interpretative methods.

49. Sir William Whitla, *Sir Isaac Newton's Daniel and the Apocalypse* (London: John Murray, 1922), 188-189 https://publicdomainreview.org/collections/sir-isaac-newtons-daniel-and-the-apocalypse-1733/

50. The Map Archive, "Papal States 1797-1870" https://www.themaparchive.com/papal-states-1797-1870.html

51. The smallest independent country (kingdom) in the world, Vatican City was established in 1929 under terms of the Lateran Treaty.

Chapter Nine

The Beast from the Sea

*"And I [he] stood upon the sand of the sea, and saw a
beast rise up out of the sea, having seven heads and ten
horns, and upon his horns ten crowns, and upon his
heads the name of blasphemy." Revelation 13:1*

Like the vision of Daniel 7, the vision of Revelation 13 depicts a
beast rising from the sea. The connection between the two visions may
be found with the fourth beast of Daniel 7 and its ten horns—one of
which replaces three of the horns and is seen possessing eyes like a man
and speaking boastful words (Daniel 7:7-8).

Early Greek manuscripts, as well as some modern Bible translations
(RSV), read "he stood," which places the dragon of Revelation 12:17 in
the presence of the beast rising up out of the sea. This beast, which has
seven heads and ten horns, is in its appearance very similar to Satan,
who is described in the book of Revelation as a great red dragon having
seven heads and ten horns (Revelation 12:3).

What is the identity of this dragon-like beast? Its physical description (Revelation 13:1-3), monstrous activities (Revelation 13:5-7), and
precarious future (Revelation 13:3-4, 8) not only point to one specific
candidate in history but reveal it to be the end-time antichrist power
whose alliance shall be with the dragon, Satan.

Much like Daniel 7, the book of Revelation provides us with eight
prophetic markers for identifying the beast from the sea.

1) Comes up after the four beasts of Daniel's vision

The beast from the sea in John's vision is described as having the combined characteristics of the four beasts of Daniel's vision (Daniel 7:2-7), thus placing it in history after the appearance of the fourth beast (the ancient Roman Empire).

"And the beast which I saw was like unto a [swift-moving] leopard, and his feet were as the [trampling] feet of a bear, and his mouth as the [roaring] mouth of a lion: and the dragon [Satan] gave him his power, and his seat, and great authority" (Revelation 13:2).

Leopard-like: moves swiftly in making war with and overcoming the saints of God.

Bear-like: tramples upon God's sanctuary and His people.

Lion-like: boasts (roars) as one having great and godlike authority.

Dragon-like: derives its power, throne, and authority from Satan.

2) Rises from the sea

With Daniel's vision of four beasts rising up out of the stormy sea, we find that these beasts represent four rising kingdoms striving for world supremacy and that the stirred-up sea represents man's strife and worldly conflicts. The beast seen rising from the sea in John's vision also represents a kingdom to come, but unlike Daniel's vision, it doesn't rise from a stirred-up sea as the result of any worldly conflict.

Perhaps John's vision is pointing forward to the time when the beast is seen ascending out of the bottomless pit or primeval sea wondrously healed (resurrected) from its deadly wound: "And I saw one of his heads as it were wounded to death; and his deadly wound was healed: and all the world wondered after the beast. And they worshipped the dragon which gave power unto the beast: and they worshipped the beast, saying, Who is like unto the beast? Who is able to make war with him?" (Revelation 13:1-4).

The reasoning for this hypothesis may be found in first understanding the Bible's use of the words "bottomless pit," which in the Greek (*abussos*) means "abyss" or "deep." In the LXX (Septuagint) it generally refers to the depths of the sea or subterranean waters (see Genesis 1:2; Job 38:30, 41:31-32). Second, when comparing Revelation 13 with the Bible's references to the angel of the bottomless pit (Revelation 9:1-2, 11), Satan at the sides of the pit (Isaiah 14:15), and the beast seen ascending out of the bottomless pit (Revelation 11:7, 17:8, 11), it appears that the beast that rises from the bottomless pit in Revelation 17 is the same beast that rises from the sea in Revelation 13. If so, then it stands to reason that the angel standing at the edge of the bottomless pit and the figure seen standing on the edge of the sea are also one and the same: Satan, also known as "Abaddon" (the destroyer) and "Apollyon" (one that exterminates or destroys), names which well suit Satan's malevolent character.

Satan, as the angel of the bottomless pit, stands in opposition to Jesus Christ, who holds ultimate power over the abyss. As for the beast that was, and is not, and shall ascend out of the bottomless pit (Revelation 17:8) it offers Satan's counterfeit to the death, burial, and resurrection of Jesus Christ.

Jesus Christ (Michael)	Satan (Abaddon-Apollyon)
Archangel (Rev. 12:7, Jude 9)	Angel of the bottomless pit (Rev. 9:11)
Shuts the bottomless pit (Rev. 20:3)	Opens the bottomless pit (Rev. 9:2)

The Lamb of God (Jesus Christ)	The Beast (the antichrist)
Was slain (Rev. 1:18; 5:6, 9)	Was smitten to death (Rev. 13:3)
Buried in earth's prison house (Eph. 4:9)	Goes into captivity (Rev. 13:10)
Resurrected from the grave (Acts 2:31)	Rises out of the pit (Rev. 17:8)

3) Receives power and great authority

Just as Jesus is the incarnate image of God and was given all power and authority from the Father, so Satan's counterfeit, the beast from the sea, is the image of the dragon (Satan) and is given the dragon's power and great authority (Revelation 13:2).

The dragon's power and authority, as represented by seven crowned heads (Revelation 12), is to be transferred to the beast's eighth head (seventh head healed) as represented by ten crowned horns (Revelation 17).

4) Speaks blasphemous words

Just like the little horn power (Daniel 7:8, 20, 25), the beast from the sea boasts great things and speaks blasphemies (Revelation 13:5-6).

5) Makes war with the saints

Just like the little horn power (Daniel 7:21), the beast from the sea makes war with the saints of the Most High (Revelation 13:7).

6) Reigns for forty-two months

Just like the little horn power (Daniel 7:25), the beast from the sea has power (temporal authority) over God's people (Revelation 13:5, 7).

John's vision of a beast rising from the sea and Daniel's vision of a little horn power both describe a kingdom speaking blasphemies, making war with the saints, and having dominion over them for 1260 days/years ("forty and two months" and "a time and times and the dividing of time").[1] The only difference is that John's vision repeats and enlarges upon Daniel's vision. Therefore, it stands to reason that they are one and the same power. As the end-time antichrist power, the beast from the sea is the second member of the dark trinity (Revelation 16:13-14).

7) Receives a deadly wound and is taken into captivity

John's vision shows us that one of the beast's seven heads was to be wounded to death by a sword (Revelation 13:3, 14). The beast's seven heads represent seven kings (kingdoms): "Five are fallen, and one is, and the other is not yet come. . . . And the beast that was, and is not, even he is the eighth, and is of the seven, and goeth into perdition" (Revelation 17:10-11).

From a historicist's point of view, the one that "is" (sixth head) most likely represents the Byzantine or Eastern Roman Empire. The five fallen kingdoms preceding it best represent Media, Babylon, Persia, Greece, and the Western Roman Empire.[2] History supports the Byzantine Empire as the sixth head or the one that "is" because the Eastern Roman Empire existed long after the fall of the Western Empire in AD 476 and witnessed the rise of a little horn kingdom in the place of the Western Empire. Therefore, it stands to reason that the seventh head best represents the Roman papacy, which rose up to power after the fall of the Western Roman Empire and reigned for 1260 years. The beast itself, which "is the eighth, and is of the seven," represents the papacy resurrected after its deadly wound is healed.

The Beast's Heads (Kings/Kingdoms)	Kingdom Ended	Revelation 17	Revelation 13
1) Media	550 BC	Five kingdoms are fallen (verse 10)	
2) Babylon	539 BC		
3) Persia	331 BC		
4) Greece	168 BC		
5) Rome (Western Empire)	AD 476		
6) Rome (Byzantine Empire)	AD 1453	And one is (verse 10)	
7) Papal Rome	AD 1870	And the other is not yet come (verse 10)	Its head is wounded to death (verse 3)
8) Papal Rome (Resurrected)	Yet to come	Ascends out of the bottomless pit; the seventh head healed (verses 8, 11)	Rises from the sea; its head is healed (verses 1, 3, 14)

History shows us that a sword came to the Roman papacy (the beast's seventh head) in 1798 when a French army under the leadership of General Berthier invaded and plundered the city of Rome and ten days later took Pope Pius VI prisoner for refusing to relinquish his temporal authority to France. The papacy's deadly wound proved fatal in 1870 when the city of Rome was surrendered to an Italian army, thus ending the last strongholds of the Roman papacy's temporal, authoritarian rule. At the same time Pope Pius IX confined himself to captivity within the Vatican walls.

"Napoleon's victory [June 1800 battle of Marengo] made him de facto ruler of Italy, but he did not interfere with Pius [VII] taking possession of Rome in July 1800. He hoped to make peace with the pope, and to incorporate the Church as an active part of his reign. . . . Unfortunately for any hopes of compromise, there were problems that would prove impossible to solve. One of these was the temporal sovereignty of the popes. This Pius absolutely would not give up: he believed that his independence as a religious leader depended on his independence as a sovereign. While he was willing to compromise on some of the outlying territories of the papal domains, he would not entertain the idea of giving up his claim to the temporal rule of the city of Rome."[3]

"With the political upheavals that followed the creation of the Roman republic in 1849, and then the kingdom of Italy in 1860, which incorporated Rome as its capital in [October] 1870, the temporal princedom of the papacy shrank to the Vatican and its immediate environs, and thus it has remained ever since."[4]

"Angered by the apparent anti-clericalism of the Italian unification engineered by Camillo Cavour and Giuseppe Garibaldi, [Pope] Pius declared he was their prisoner and from 1871 confined himself as such to the Vatican."[5]

"At that time [the fall of the City of Rome in 1870] the pope became a prisoner of the Vatican until the solution of the 'Roman Question' in 1929."[6]

8) Healed from its deadly wound

After the king of Italy stripped the Roman pontiff of his temporal power and the territories he controlled (the Papal States), the pope's rule and authority were in essence limited to the Vatican. However, Bible prophecy reveals to us that the beast's deadly wound was to be healed: "And I saw one of his heads as it were wounded to death; and his deadly wound was healed: and all the world wondered after the beast" (Revelation 13:3). History shows us that the beast's deadly wound was at least partially healed when under the Lateran Treaty of 1929, Vatican City was officially recognized by Italy as an independent and sovereign nation (kingdom). The Holy See was recognized as its seat of government, with its authority residing with the acting Roman pontiff.

"This situation was finally resolved on February 11, 1929, in an agreement between the Holy See and the Kingdom of Italy. The [Lateran] treaty was signed by Benito Mussolini and Pietro Cardinal Gasparri in behalf of King Victor Emmanuel III and Pope Pius XI (1922-1939), respectively. The Lateran Treaty and the Concordat established the independent State of the Vatican City and granted Catholicism special status in Italy. In 1984, a new concordat between the Holy See and Italy modified certain provisions of the earlier treaty, including the position of Catholicism as the Italian state religion."[7]

"The fall of Napoleon [III] permitted Victor Emmanuel to seize Rome in 1870. However, Pius IX refused to recognize the loss of temporal power and became a prisoner in the Vatican; his successors followed his example. The so-called Roman Question was only resolved in 1929 by the Lateran Treaty, which, among other things, established Vatican City."[8]

Let us remember that the beast's deadly head wound, which occurred in 1798, didn't prove fatal until 1870. Therefore, the same may be said of the healing of the head wound, which began in 1929 but shall not be fully healed until the time predicted when "all the world wondered after the beast" (Revelation 13:3).

Summary:

Enraged with the woman and ready to make war with the remnant of her offspring who keep the commandments of God and hold to the testimony of Jesus, the dragon (Satan) is seen in John the Revelator's vision standing in the presence of a beast rising up out of the primeval sea (abyss or bottomless pit). This dragon-like beast, whose power, throne, and great authority come from Satan himself, is historically the same little horn power that reigned for 42 months (1260 years) until its deadly wound in 1798 proved fatal in 1870. Yet as Bible prophecy predicted, this dragon-like beast found new life when Vatican City became an independent and sovereign nation with the signing of the

Lateran Treaty in 1929. Today, this resurrected dragon-like beast or little horn power continues to strive for world supremacy. Yet the book of Revelation tells us that in the end, this worldly power shall be strongly judged by God and cast into the lake of fire or second death along with the dragon, the false prophet, and those whose names are not written in the Lamb's book of life.

> *"The beast that thou sawest was, and is not; and shall ascend out of the bottomless pit, and go to perdition: and they that dwell on the earth shall wonder, whose names were not written in the [Lamb's] book of life from the foundation of the world, when they behold the beast that was, and is not, and yet is." Revelation 17:8*

Notes:

1. "A time and times and the dividing of time" = 3½ years, 42 months, or 1260 prophetic days/literal years. See Principle 4 in Chapter 4 for more information.

2   The Medes were defeated by the Persian king Cyrus in 550 BC. (Some historians place this event in 549 BC.) The Medes and Persians together went on to defeat Babylon in 539 BC.

3. Susan Vandiver Nicassio, *Imperial City: Rome under Napoleon* (Chicago, IL: The Univ. of Chicago Press, 2009), 26

4. P. G. Maxwell-Stuart, *Chronicle of the Popes* (London: Thames & Hudson, 1997), 218

5. Ibid.

6. Richard P. McBrien, *The Harper Collins Encyclopedia of Catholicism* (New York: HarperCollins Publishers Inc., 1995), 1295

7. Frank Kaufman, ed., *New World Encyclopedia,* "Vatican City" http://www.newworldencyclopedia.org

8. *The Columbia Electronic Encyclopedia*, 6th ed. (New York: Columbia Univ. Press, 2013), "Papal States" https://encyclopedia2.thefreedictionary.com/Papal+territory

Chapter Ten

The Spirit and Power of Elijah

"Behold, I will send you Elijah the prophet before the coming of the great and dreadful day of the Lord: and he shall turn the heart of the fathers to the children, and the heart of the children to their fathers." Malachi 4:5-6

In the days of King Ahab,[1] much of Israel had wandered away from the one true God and were led into worshiping the false gods of Baal and Ashtoreth. Israel's wanderings were the direct result of King Ahab's wanderings and the influences of his idolatrous foreign wife, Jezebel, who as a priestess of Baal kept company with 450 prophets of Baal at her dinner table. However, Elijah the Tishbite, who walked with the God of Abraham, Isaac, and Jacob, was given the daunting task of bringing Israel, God's chosen people, back to the one true God.

With most of Israel living in national apostasy and bound up in the sins of their king, God sent Elijah to King Ahab with a prophetic message: "As the Lord God of Israel liveth, before whom I stand, there shall not be dew nor rain these years, but according to my word" (1 Kings 17:1). With God's judgment and curse pronounced upon the land, both Israel and its king, who had put their faith in the god of Baal for rain, were now destined to see their folly in wandering after strange gods.

Only after three years of severe drought and famine did God send Elijah back to King Ahab. Elijah called for the prophets of Baal and the people of Israel to gather at Mount Carmel. It was here on Mount Carmel that Elijah's charge was given to Israel as to whom they would worship: "How long halt ye between two opinions? If the Lord be God, follow him: but if Baal, then follow him. . . . And the God that answereth by fire, let him be God. And all the people answered and said, It is well spoken" (1 Kings 18:21-24).

With the people gathered, Elijah called on the prophets of Baal to build an altar and to prepare a bull for sacrifice to their god. From morning until early evening, the prophets of Baal called upon their god to answer their chanting, dancing, prophesying, and bloodletting, yet they were met only with silence.

With evening approaching, Elijah called the people to himself and afterwards repaired the broken-down altar of the Lord, dug a trench around it, and prepared a bull for sacrifice. Then, as an act of assurance that no trickery was to be used in kindling a fire, he ordered twelve barrels of water to be poured over the sacrifice and the wood underneath it. At the appointed time for the evening sacrifice, Elijah called upon the Lord in prayer: "Lord God of Abraham, Isaac, and of Israel, let it be known this day that thou art God in Israel, and that I am thy servant, and that I have done all these things at thy word. Hear me, O Lord, hear me, that this people may know that thou art the Lord God, and that thou hast turned their heart back again" (1 Kings 18:36-37).

The Scriptures tell us that not only did the Lord God answer Elijah's prayer with fire from heaven, but the fire consumed the sacrifice, the wood, the water, and even the stones of the altar, leaving no doubt in anyone's mind that Elijah's God was the Lord God of heaven and earth. "And when all the people saw it, they fell on their faces; and they said, The Lord, He is God; the Lord, He is God" (1 Kings 18:39, NASB).

Elijah's Mission and Message in the Last Days

In reference to Elijah's mission and message to Israel, the prophet Malachi tells us that God will once again send Elijah to restore the hearts of His people to Himself. "Behold, I will send you Elijah the prophet before the coming of the great and dreadful day of the Lord: and he shall turn the heart of the fathers to the children, and the heart of the children to their fathers, lest I come and smite the earth with a curse" (Malachi 4:5-6).

What is interesting about this prophecy is that Jesus used it to point His disciples to John the Baptist, who as God's messenger was called to "make ready a people prepared for the Lord" (Luke 1:17). Yet when examining this prophecy, it is evident that Malachi is speaking of a prophetic messenger who, like John, is to help make ready a people before the Lord Jesus' second coming.

Knowing that the great and dreadful day of the Lord (Jesus' return) has not yet come, we need to ask ourselves, Has God's messenger already come in this last dispensation? And if so, then what is his special message for us today?

Standing at the opposite poles of Christendom, I dare to say, are two worldwide movements that best answer these questions. Their remarkable similarities and striking differences, when compared and examined, should leave little doubt in anyone's mind as to which is God's messenger and which is Satan's counterfeit.

Both the Church of Jesus Christ of Latter-day Saints[2] and the Seventh-day Adventist Church[3] believe that God has called them to be His prophetic messenger in this last dispensation. In other words, both of these worldwide movements claim to have the mission and message of Elijah by divine appointment.

The Angel Moroni and the Golden Plates (Book of Mormon)[4]

Latter-day Saints believe their calling comes from Joseph Smith's visitation with the angel Moroni,[5] who quoted a variation of Malachi's prophecy to him and informed Joseph Smith that this prediction was about to be fulfilled. "For behold, the day cometh that shall burn as an oven, and all the proud, yea, and all that do wickedly shall burn as stubble; for they that come shall burn them, saith the Lord of Hosts, that it shall leave them neither root nor branch. Behold, I will reveal unto you the Priesthood, by the hand of Elijah the prophet, before the coming of the great and dreadful day of the Lord. And he shall plant in the hearts of the children the promises made to the fathers, and the hearts of the children shall turn to their fathers. If it were not so, the whole earth would be utterly wasted at his coming."[6]

One week after the dedicatory service of the Kirtland Temple (the first of now 168 dedicated Latter-day Saint temples around the world), Malachi's prophecy, as prophesied by Moroni, came to pass when the prophet Elijah visited Joseph Smith and Oliver Cowdery in the Kirtland Temple.[7]

On this day [April 3, 1836] Elijah appeared to Joseph Smith and Oliver Cowdery in the Kirtland Temple and there conferred upon them his priesthood, which is the power to bind, or seal, on earth and in heaven. The keys of this priesthood were held by Elijah, to whom the Lord gave power over the elements as well as over men, with the authority to seal for time and eternity on the righteous all the ordinances pertaining to the fullness of salvation.[8]

Having received the keys from Elijah for sealing on earth and in heaven all the ordinances ministered in the temple, the Church today fulfills the role of Elijah in turning "the heart of the fathers to the children, and the heart of the children to their fathers" by sealing families (both the living and the dead) for time and all eternity to come.

The Mighty Angel and the Open Book

Seventh-day Adventists believe their calling comes directly from Jesus as prophesied in the Book of Revelation.

"And I saw another mighty angel come down from heaven, clothed with a cloud: and a rainbow was upon his head, and his face was as it were the sun, and his feet as pillars of fire: and he had in his hand a little book open: and he set his right foot upon the sea, and his left foot on the earth. . . . And the voice which I heard from heaven spake unto me again, and said, Go and take the little book which is open in the hand of the angel which standeth upon the sea and upon the earth. And I went unto the angel, and said unto him, Give me the little book. And he said unto me, Take it, and eat it up; and it shall make thy belly bitter, but it shall be in thy mouth sweet as honey. And I took the little book out of the angel's hand, and ate it up; and it was in my mouth sweet as honey: and as soon as I had eaten it, my belly was bitter. And he said unto me, Thou must prophesy again before many peoples, and nations, and tongues, and kings" (Revelation 10:1-11).

The mighty angel is symbolic of a heavenly messenger and is the same figure mentioned in Revelation 1 and 4 and in Ezekiel 1. The open book represents the prophetic book of Daniel as being unsealed (open to human understanding). John's consumption of the book, which was sweet to the mouth but bitter to the stomach, equates to the experiences of the Millerite "Advent" movement. Based upon the timeline prophecies of Daniel, they believed with a sweetness of joy that Jesus' coming was soon, yet they were bitterly disappointed when He didn't come as anticipated in the fall of 1844, marking their "Great Disappointment."

Out of the Great Disappointment rose a small flock of Adventist believers who never gave up their hope in Jesus' coming and through collective prayer and Bible study found the answer to their great disappointment. In 1863, they became legally organized and are known today as the Seventh-day Adventists. Claiming to meet the identifying marks of the persecuted woman's offspring (Revelation 12:17) who keep the commandments of God and hold to the testimony of Jesus (the spirit of prophecy), they see their calling as described in this prophecy: "And he said unto me, Thou must prophesy again before many peoples, and nations, and tongues, and kings" (Revelation 10:11).

"The Scriptures testify that one of the gifts of the Holy Spirit is prophecy. This gift is an identifying mark of the remnant church and we believe it was manifested in the ministry of Ellen G. White. Her writings speak with prophetic authority and provide comfort, guidance, instruction, and correction to the church. They also make clear that the Bible is the standard by which all teaching and experience must be tested."[9]

"The universal church is composed of all who truly believe in Christ, but in the last days, a time of widespread apostasy, a remnant has been called out to keep the commandments of God and the faith of Jesus. This remnant announces the arrival of the judgment hour, proclaims salvation through Christ, and heralds the approach of His second advent. This proclamation is symbolized by the three angels of Revelation 14; it coincides with the work of judgment in heaven and results in a work of repentance and reform on earth. Every believer is called to have a personal part in this worldwide witness."[10]

The Angel's Message

As for Elijah's mission and message in preparing the way before Christ's soon coming, both movements lay claim to Revelation 14:6-7 as the prophetic basis for their mission and message to the world.

"And I saw another angel fly in the midst of heaven, having the everlasting gospel to preach unto them that dwell on the earth, and to every nation, and kindred, and tongue, and people, saying with a loud voice, Fear God, and give glory to him; for the hour of his judgment is come: and worship him that made heaven, and earth, and the sea, and the fountains of waters" (Revelation 14:6-7).

Latter-day Saints believe that the angel represents the angel Moroni and that the everlasting gospel to be preached to the world is the fullness of the gospel of Jesus Christ, which includes the Book of Mormon. The angel's loud voice is heaven's proclamation and warning to the world that the fullness of the gospel of Jesus Christ has been restored upon the earth and that God's judgment is close at hand. In addition to preaching the everlasting gospel (the Book of Mormon), the mission of the Church is to perform the ordinances of the gospel in perfecting the saints and redeeming the dead. Together, these three principles constitute God's mission and special message to the world.

"We are impressed that the mission of the Church is threefold:

To proclaim the gospel of the Lord Jesus Christ to every nation, kindred, tongue, and people;

To perfect the Saints by preparing them to receive the ordinances of the gospel and by instruction and discipline to gain exaltation;

To redeem the dead by performing vicarious ordinances of the gospel for those who have lived on the earth.

All three are part of one work; to assist our Father in Heaven and his Son, Jesus Christ, in their grand and glorious mission 'to bring to pass the immortality and eternal life of man.'"[11]

Seventh-day Adventists believe that the angel is symbolic of a prophetic movement and that the everlasting gospel to be preached to all the world is the same gospel that was preached during apostolic times—a gospel full of light and truth as found in the Bible and the Bible alone. As for the angel's loud voice, it is heaven's voice of warning to all that He who is worthy of all honor, glory, and worship is to judge His people (both the dead and the living) before the great and awful day of the Lord. In addition to preaching the fullness of the everlasting gospel and proclaiming God's pre-advent judgment (1844 to present),

Seventh-day Adventists believe that it is their mission to proclaim the second and third angel's messages (Revelation 14:8-12), which together define and form the Church's mission and special message to the world.

The Seventh-day Adventist Church's officially stated mission is: "Make disciples of Jesus Christ who live as His loving witnesses and proclaim to all people the everlasting gospel of the Three Angels' Messages in preparation for His soon return (Matt. 28:18-20, Acts 1:8, Rev. 14:6-12)."[12]

"As Seventh-day Adventists, we accept the Bible as the foundation for all our beliefs and see in its pages our unique prophetic identity and mission. . . . We are to be a peculiar people, God's remnant people, to lift up Christ, His righteousness, His three angels' messages of Revelation 14, and His soon coming."[13]

For a more complete overview and understanding of the similarities and differences between these two Elijah-like candidates, see Appendices D and E.

The False Prophet's Mission and Message in the Last Days

As we approach the last days of earth's history, Satan will increasingly work his mastery of deceptions and lies. Cloaked as being from God, his grand end-time schemes shall if possible deceive even the very elect. During the time of the latter rain (the last great spiritual awakening), Satan, in alliance with the beast and the false prophet, shall counteract God's wondrous works of spiritual revival with wonder-working miracles of his own. These lying wonders are cunningly designed to help draw the world away from the one true God and His eternal truths. "And I saw three unclean spirits like frogs come out of the mouth of the dragon [Satan], and out the mouth of the beast, and out of the mouth of the false prophet. For they are the spirits of devils, working miracles, which go forth unto the kings of the earth and the whole world, to gather them to the battle of that great day of God Almighty" (Revelation 16:13-14). With much of the world—Christians included—believing that man's soul is immortal, one of Satan's grand end-time deceptions may be a false resurrection of departed souls. The basis for this counterfeit resurrection comes from the biblical account in which a portion of the righteous dead came out of the grave at Christ's resurrection (Matthew 27:52-53). As a living testimony of Jesus' resurrection power and as first fruits of the resurrection to come, they bore witness that Jesus is Lord and Savior! As for the purpose of a counterfeit resurrection, Satan and his false witnesses (devils masquerading as resurrected human beings) would be able to bear false testimony and give false security as to what is required for man's salvation. "Now the Spirit speaketh expressly, that in the latter times some shall depart from the faith, giving heed to seducing spirits, and doctrines of devils" (1 Timothy 4:1).

Will Satan himself, the prince of darkness, masquerade upon the earth as "an angel of light" (2 Corinthians 11:14) and thus appear to the world as the promised messiah to come? Time will tell, but one thing is for sure: We will know the lying serpent of old by his crafty words. If he speaks not according to the straight and full testimony of God's Word, the Old and New Testaments, which are in harmony with each other, then we will know him to be the devil and father of lies!

Along with the beast and the spirits of devils working miracles and propagating lies, the Bible warns us of another false witness, the false prophet, who in the last days shall perform great signs and wonders (miracles), "so that he maketh fire come down from heaven on the earth in the sight of men" (Revelation 13:13). With so many—Christians included—putting their faith in "seeing is believing" rather than "the substance of things hoped for, [and] the evidence of things not seen" (Hebrews 11:1), the time of this great deception shall surely come to pass when Satan's lying wonder of bringing down fire from heaven will be seen by many as a true sign and ominous declaration from God.

Why does God allow Satan to bring down strange fire—a lie between heaven and earth—in the sight of men? The answer can be found in the book of Deuteronomy: "If a prophet or a dreamer of dreams arises among you and gives you a sign or a wonder, and the sign or the wonder comes true, concerning which he spoke to you, saying, 'Let us go after other gods (whom you have not known) and let us serve them,' you shall not listen to the words of that prophet or that dreamer of dreams; for the Lord your God is testing you to find out if you love the Lord your God with all your heart and with all your soul. You shall follow the Lord your God and fear Him; and you shall keep His commandments,[14] listen to His voice, serve Him, and cling to Him" (Deuteronomy 13:1-4, NASB).

In other words, God's purposes are met in the testing of people's hearts to distinguish "between him that serveth God and him that serveth him not" (Malachi 3:18). Interestingly enough, in the last days, the same test will be given to God's people as was presented in the days of Elijah: "If the Lord be God, follow him [by keeping His commandments]: but if Baal, then follow him. . . . And the God that answereth by fire, let him be God" (1 Kings 18:21-24). The difference is that it will be the false prophet calling and the dragon answering with a most wondrous lie.

Knowing that Satan has the power to bring down fire from heaven (Job 1:16), we need to cling to the safeguard of God's Word as our rule of faith and our standard by which we test everything. By doing so, we may know and avoid the devil's trickery and deadly deceptions. "Beloved, believe not every spirit, but try the spirits whether they are of God: because many false prophets are gone out into the world" (1 John 4:1).

Summary:
The prophet Malachi tells us that before the Lord's return, Elijah will come to turn back the hearts of the fathers to the children and the children to their fathers. Standing in the world today are two worldwide movements, The Church of Jesus Christ of Latter-day Saints and the Seventh-day Adventist Church, which in the spirit and power of Elijah[15] both claim to be God's prophetic messenger in these latter days. These worldwide movements exhibit some similarities, including shared Bible texts as the basis of their mission and message. Yet examining their testimony under the lenses of the Old and New Testament causes one to wonder: If one is truly God's prophetic messenger today, then the other must surely be Satan's counterfeit and the false prophet warned of in the book of Revelation.

"For there shall arise false Christs, and false prophets,
and shall shew great signs and wonders; insomuch that,
if it were possible, they shall deceive the very elect."
Matthew 24:24

Notes:

1.   Seventh king of Israel after the monarchy split; reigned from 874-53 BC

2.   See Appendix D: Beliefs of the Latter-day Saints (Mormons)

3.   See Appendix E: Beliefs of the Seventh-day Adventists

4.   Joseph Smith translated the Book of Mormon from a set of golden plates received from the angel Moroni.

5.   The angel Moroni is a heavenly being who once lived upon the earth as a Nephite prophet, according to the Book of Mormon.

6.   Joseph Smith, *Joseph Smith—History* 1:36-39
https://www.lds.org/scriptures/pgp/js-h/1?lang=eng

7.   A vision manifested to Joseph Smith and Oliver Cowdery (*Doctrine and Covenants* 110:13-16).

8.   Joseph Fielding Smith, "The Coming of Elijah," *Ensign Magazine* (January 1972)
https://www.lds.org/study/ensign/1972/01/the-coming-of-elijah?lang=eng

9.   Seventh-day Adventist Fundamental Beliefs: The Gift of Prophecy
https://www.adventist.org/en/beliefs/church/the-gift-of-prophecy/

10. Seventh-day Adventist Fundamental Beliefs: The Remnant and Its Mission
https://www.adventist.org/en/beliefs/church/the-remnant-and-its-mission/

11. Spencer W. Kimball and Edward L. Kimball, *The Teachings of Spencer W. Kimball* (Salt Lake City, UT: Deseret Book, 1982), 434

12. Seventh-day Adventist Church official mission statement (October 15, 2018)
https://adventist.org/en/information/official-statements/statements/

13. Ted N. C. Wilson, "Go Forward," *Adventist Review Magazine* (July 20, 2010)
https://www.adventistreview.org/2010-1526-2

14. Matthew 22:36-40 (God's Ten Commandments as reflected in our love for God and man)

15. Luke 1:17 (Elias is a variant of the English word Elijah.)

Chapter Eleven

The Beast from the Earth

*"And I beheld another beast coming up out of the earth;
and he had two horns like a lamb, and he spake as a
dragon. . . . He maketh fire come down from heaven on
the earth in the sight of men, and deceiveth them that
dwell on the earth by the means of those miracles which
he had power to do in the sight of the beast."*
Revelation 13:11-14

In addition to the dragon-like sea beast, John saw in vision a second beast, but instead of coming up out of the sea or bottomless pit (resurrected from its deadly wound), it is seen coming up out of the earth. John's description of this second beast as having two horns like a lamb (Jesus) and speaking like a dragon (Satan) reveals it to be a deceptive foe—a wolf in sheep's clothing. Furthermore, by performing great signs and wonders, it shall deceive many, including, if possible, God's people in the last days.

Who or what is this mysterious beast that rises up after the dragon-like sea beast receives its deadly wound in 1798? The book of Revelation provides us with six prophetic identifying markers.

1) Rises from the earth

In the Old Testament story of King Saul and the witch of Endor (1 Samuel 28), we find a woman medium conjuring up an evil spirit. "Then said the woman, Whom shall I bring up unto thee? And he [Saul] said, Bring me up [the prophet] Samuel" (1 Samuel 28:11). Describing the familiar spirit, the woman said to Saul, "I see a divine being coming up out of the earth" (1 Samuel 28:13, NASB).

Here is presented one of Satan's greatest lies perpetuated down through the ages: the dead can speak to the living. The occult practices of both ancient and modern spiritualism teach that man can have communication with the departed spirits of the dead, which is an abomination unto the Lord. "And the soul that turneth after such as have familiar spirits, and after wizards, to go a whoring after them, I will even set my face against that soul, and will cut him off from among his people" (Leviticus 20:6). "So Saul died for his transgression which he committed against the Lord, even against the word of the Lord, which he kept not, and also for asking counsel of one that had a familiar spirit, to enquire of it" (1 Chronicles 10:13).

In light of the witch's description of a false spirit coming up out of the earth and impersonating the dead prophet Samuel, John's description of a beast (kingdom) coming out of the earth may indicate a rising kingdom based on the principles of spiritualism. Modern spiritualism is said to have risen up in America during the mid-nineteenth century, with the Fox sisters as its first converts.[1] Yet as a spiritual movement, it lacks the hierarchy, governance, or order that would normally be associated with a kingdom.

According to Brigham Young, president and prophet of The Church of Jesus Christ of Latter-day Saints (1847-77), this spiritualist movement is the devil's counterfeit to Mormonism, which was restored upon the earth in 1830. Young stated:

> We are accused of being nothing more nor less than a people possessing what they term the higher order of Spiritualism. Whenever I see this in print, or hear it spoken, "You are right," say I. Yes, we belong to that higher order of Spiritualism . . . and there is quite a difference between the two [spiritual systems]. One forms a perfect chain, the links of which cannot be separated; one has perfect order, laws, rules, regulations, organization; it forms, fashions, makes, creates, produces, protects and holds in existence the inhabitants of the earth in

> a pure and holy form of government, preparatory to their entering the kingdom of Heaven. The other is a rope of sand; it is disjointed, jargon, confusion, discord, everybody receiving revelation to suit himself. . . . There is no order, no organization; it cannot be reduced to a system, it is uncertainty. That is the difference between the two spiritual systems—yes, this is the higher order of spiritualism, to be led, governed and controlled by law, and that, too, the law of heaven that governs and controls the Gods and the angels.[2]

What president and prophet Young is exclaiming, and what Bible prophecy supports, is that without organization, law, and order, spiritualism cannot be the beast (kingdom) seen rising up out of the earth. Mormonism, on the other hand, which is described as the "higher order of spiritualism," is proclaimed by the LDS Church to be "the Lord's kingdom once again established on the earth, preparatory to the second coming of the Messiah."[3]

Emma Hardinge Britten (1823-1899), who was an advocate and practitioner of the nineteenth-century Spiritualist movement, is widely credited today with defining the **Seven Principles of Spiritualism**.[4] Both the National Spiritualist Association of Churches in the United States and the Spiritualist National Union in the United Kingdom affirm these seven defining principles, which are:

1) **The Fatherhood of God** (God is our heavenly father).
2) **The Brotherhood of Man** (we are all members of the same divine family).
3) **The Communion of Spirits and the Ministry of Angels** (we can communicate with departed spirits that minister to the living).
4) **The Continuous Existence of the Human Soul** (immortality of the soul).
5) **Personal Responsibility** (free agency).
6) **Compensation and Retribution Hereafter for All the Good and Evil Deeds Done on Earth** (for good or for evil, our earthly works earn for us our eternal reward).
7) **Eternal Progress Open to Every Human Soul** (to become as God is).[5]

It is worth noting that The Church of Jesus Christ of Latter-day Saints not only affirms these seven core principles in its teachings and testimonies, but, as stated by President Young, is an organized form of modern spiritualism syncretized with the features and functionality of Christianity.

Is America the birthplace of this beast? Bible prophecy tells us that the second beast rises from the earth and not the sea, which would suggest that it is not in any way associated with the first beast from the sea (the Roman papacy). Mormonism meets this peculiarity in that it was founded in America (April 6, 1830, Fayette, New York) and is the only new Christian tradition that is totally separate from Roman Catholicism as well as from Protestantism, which rose out of Roman Catholicism in the Old World.

Joseph Smith, who was one of the founding members as well as the first president and prophet of the Church, states in his personal testimony that in his search to know which if any church to join, he was met with Satan's attack as well as God's deliverance and divine answer. (For Joseph Smith's more complete testimony, see Appendix D.)

"My object in going to inquire of the Lord was to know which of all the [Christian] sects was right, that I might know which to join."[6]

"I was answered that I must join none of them, for they are all wrong; and the Personage who addressed me said that all their creeds [doctrines or beliefs] were an abomination in his sight; that those professors were all corrupt."[7]

LDS Church teachings reaffirm Joseph Smith's testimony and belief that The Church of Jesus Christ of Latter-day Saints is not an extension of the Protestant Reformation movement but the true and living church (as during apostolic times) restored upon the earth today.

"He [Joseph Smith] was told in this [first] vision that the true Church of Jesus Christ that had been established in New Testament times, and which had administered the fullness of the gospel, was no longer on the earth . . . and that through him the Church of Jesus Christ would be restored to the earth."[8]

"And also those to whom these commandments were given, might have power to lay the foundation of this church, and to bring it forth out of obscurity and out of darkness, the only true and living church upon the face of the whole earth, with which I, the Lord, am well pleased, speaking unto the church collectively and not individually."[9]

2) Has two horns like a lamb

Horns in Bible prophecy symbolize kings, kingdoms, and powers of authority. The symbol of the Lamb in the book of Revelation points to Jesus Christ, who alone is King of kings and great high priest after the order of Melchizedek (Hebrews 5:10). Melchizedek was a type of Christ (Zechariah 6:12-13) who held the dual office of both king and high priest during the patriarchal time of Abraham.

The beast's "two horns like a lamb" may therefore symbolize a Christlike kingdom upon the earth that governs both the political and the ecclesiastical affairs of men.

Will America one day be ruled and governed as an ecclesiastical-political kingdom under the royal-priesthood authority of Melchizedek? Time will tell, but one thing is for sure: The Church of Jesus Christ of Latter-day Saints, which rose up in America, believes that during the millennium, when Christ is once again upon the earth, the kingdom of God shall be both an ecclesiastical and political kingdom ruled and governed by the hierarchy of the LDS Church. Furthermore, if LDS history is any indication of their anticipated future, then the president of the LDS Church may once again, if not already, hold the dual governing offices of both high priest and king.

"The Church of Jesus Christ of Latter-day Saints is the kingdom of God on the earth, but it is at present limited to an ecclesiastical kingdom. During the Millennium, the kingdom of God will be both political and ecclesiastical."[10]

"The Kingdom of God in the millennium will be both an ecclesiastical and political kingdom ruled and governed by the LDS Church. Following the resurrection of mankind, the Kingdom of God is the celestial kingdom and does not include the terrestrial or telestial kingdoms (*Mormon Doctrine*, 415-417)."[11]

"After Christ comes, all the peoples of the earth will be subject to him, but there will be multitudes of people on the face of the earth who will not be members of the Church; yet all will have to be obedient to the laws of the kingdom of God, for it will have dominion upon the whole face of the earth. These people will be subject to the political government, even though they are not members of the ecclesiastical kingdom which is the Church.

"This government which embraces all the peoples of the earth, both in and out of the Church, is also sometimes spoken of as the kingdom of God, because the people are subject to the kingdom of God which Christ will set up; but they have their [free] agency and thousands will not be members of the Church until they are converted; yet at the same time they will be subject to the theocratic rule."[12]

3) Speaks as a dragon

To understand how the beast from the earth shall speak as a dragon, we need only to examine the Scriptures. In the Gospel of John, the dragon (Satan) is described by Jesus as being the father of lies: "When he speaketh a lie, he speaketh of his own; for he is a liar, and the father of it" (John 8:44). The book of Revelation further describes Satan's spoken lies: "And I saw three unclean spirits like frogs come out of the mouth of the dragon, and out of the mouth of the beast, and out of the mouth of the false prophet. For they are the spirits of devils, working miracles" (Revelation 16:13-14). It should be no wonder, then, that like "the father of lies," the beast shall also speak lying wonders (miracles).

4) Exercises the same power (authority) as the beast from the sea

Another identifying mark of the beast from the earth is that it shall exercise the same power as the beast from the sea. In order to understand what this power or authority is, we must examine the authority of the beast from the sea—the Roman papacy.

"And I say also unto thee, That thou art Peter, and upon this rock I will build my church; and the gates of hell shall not prevail against it. And I will give unto thee the keys of the kingdom of heaven: and whatsoever thou shalt bind on earth shall be bound in heaven: and whatsoever thou shalt loose on earth shall be loosed in heaven" (Matthew 16:18-19). As an ecclesiastical system of governance, the Roman papacy claims that its authority rests with the apostle Peter, who established the apostolic priesthood in Rome, and that its apostolic authority continues with Peter's successors, the bishops of Rome (popes), who have been given the priesthood keys of God's kingdom here on earth and in heaven.

The LDS Church also claims apostolic authority. According to Joseph Smith, the authority was restored upon the earth when Joseph and his friend Oliver Cowdery were visited by John the Baptist and later by the resurrected apostles Peter, James, and John. By way of these heavenly visitors and the laying on of hands, both the Aaronic and Melchizedek priesthoods were restored. Today the keys of the Melchizedek priesthood are always held by the twelve modern apostles of the LDS Church, but only the presiding high priest (the president and prophet of the Church) administers all the keys for the spiritual and temporal affairs of the Church (the kingdom of God upon the earth).

"The priesthood of God is the ministering arm of the Lord's work on earth. It is noteworthy that the [Roman] Catholic Church and The Church of Jesus Christ of Latter-day Saints are the only Christian institutions that claim to hold the authoritative priesthood of Jesus Christ, both declaring an unbroken succession of apostolic authority."[13]

5) Performs miraculous signs and wonders

In the last days, the beast from the earth, also known as the false prophet in the book of Revelation, shall perform great signs and wonders. "He doeth great wonders, so that he maketh fire come down from heaven on the earth in the sight of men" (Revelation 13:13). Here is presented the third member and false witness of the dark trinity (Revelation 16:13-14, 19:20), who "after the working of Satan with all power and signs and lying wonders" (2 Thessalonians 2:9) shall deceive many by calling down fire from heaven. Seeing this miraculous sign and believing it to be a declaration from God, many shall come to take their stand under the popular banner of worshipping the beast and its image.

Will The Church of Jesus Christ of Latter-day Saints one day fulfill Bible prophecy and through its living prophet call down fire from heaven? Time will tell, but one thing is for sure: the "strange fire" seen coming down out of heaven will not be from God!

6) Gives life to the formed image of the beast

The beast from the earth influences earth's inhabitants to set up an image in the likeness of the beast from the sea (Revelation 13:14-15). Mormon interpretation of Bible prophecy declares that the kingdom of God upon the earth following Jesus' return will be a religious-political kingdom governed by The Church of Jesus Christ of Latter-day Saints. This could accurately be described as an "image" or likeness of the Roman papacy. For a better understanding of the end-time theocratic government envisioned by Mormon teaching, see Appendix C.

This formed image will speak a death decree to all those who don't worship the beast and its image. In Daniel 3 we find a similar dire situation where those who didn't bow down and worship the golden image that King Nebuchadnezzar had set up—an image that reflected his kingdom being an everlasting kingdom upon the earth—were subject to death. Those who refuse to bow to the end-time image of the beast will have to pass through a fiery trial similar to that of Daniel's three friends, not knowing if God will save them from certain death.

Summary:

The book of Revelation speaks of two beasts (kingdoms) in alliance with the dragon (Satan) in the last days. The first is seen coming up out the sea or bottomless pit, whereas the second is seen rising out of the earth. In John's description of this second kingdom, its lamblike horns show it to be Christlike (having the nominal characteristics of Christianity), yet its deceptive works (miracles and lying wonders) reveal its inward nature (spiritualism) to be that of the devil. This kingdom may be best identified with The Church of Jesus Christ of Latter-day Saints, which as a spiritualistic kingdom claims the same apostolic authority as the first beast, yet distinguishes itself as the kingdom of God "restored" upon the earth today.

> *"Beware of false prophets, which come to you in sheep's*
> *clothing, but inwardly they are ravening wolves."*
> *Matthew 7:15*

Notes:

1. Wikipedia, "Fox Sisters"

https://en.m.wikipedia.org/wiki/Fox_sisters

2. Brigham Young, "The Word of Wisdom—Spiritualism," *Journal of Discourses,* vol. 13 (October 30, 1870): 281

https://archive.org/details/journaldiscours00grimgoog/page/n292

3. *The Book of Mormon: Another Testament of Jesus Christ* (Salt Lake City, UT: The Church of Jesus Christ of Latter-Day Saints, 1981), Introduction to the Book of Mormon

4. Wikipedia, "Emma Hardinge Britten"

https://en.wikipedia.org/wiki/Emma_Hardinge_Britten

5. Spiritualists' National Union, "7 Principles"

https://www.snu.org.uk/7-principles

6. Joseph Smith, *Joseph Smith—History* 1:18

https://www.lds.org/scriptures/pgp/js-h/1?lang=eng

7. Smith, *Joseph Smith—History* 1:19

8. *The Doctrine and Covenants of the Church of Jesus Christ of Latter-Day Saints* (Salt Lake City, UT: The Church of Jesus Christ of Latter-day Saints, 1981), "Introduction to the Doctrine and Covenants"

9. *Doctrine and Covenants* 1:30

10. The Church of Jesus Christ of Latter-day Saints/Guide to the Scriptures/Kingdom of God or Kingdom of Heaven

https://www.lds.org/scriptures/gs/kingdom-of-god-or-kingdom-of-heaven?lang=eng&letter=K

11. Mormonism Research Ministry/A-Z definitions of LDS terminology/Kingdom of God

https://www.mrm.org/kingdom-of-god

12. Bruce R. McConkie, ed., *Doctrines of Salvation—Sermons and Writings of Joseph Fielding Smith,* vol. 1 (Salt Lake City, UT: Deseret Book, 1954), 141

13. Eric Shuster, *Catholic Roots, Mormon Harvest* (Springville, UT: Cedar Fort, Inc., 2009), 122

Section III

Crises and Crowns

Chapter Twelve

The Three Angels' Message

"And the smoke of their torment ascendeth up for ever and ever: and they have no rest day nor night, who worship the beast and his image, and whosoever receiveth the mark of his name. Here is the patience of the saints: here are they that keep the commandments of God, and the faith of Jesus." Revelation 14:11-12

The message of the three angels in Revelation 14 is God's latter-day message being heralded to His people living in what the prophet Daniel referred to as "the time of the end." Each angel's proclamation has its prophetic place in history, yet they form a threefold message in proclaiming God's everlasting truth, mercy, and justice for all.

First Angel

"And I saw another angel fly in the midst of heaven, having the everlasting gospel to preach unto them that dwell on the earth, . . . saying with a loud voice, Fear God, and give glory to him; for the hour of his judgment is come: and worship him that made heaven, and earth, and the sea, and the fountains of waters." Revelation 14:6-7

The first angel's message not only reminds God's covenant-keeping people of the everlasting gospel to be preached to all the world but announces a pre-advent judgment to come upon everyone who has ever claimed to be a member of God's people. The first angel's announcement of a pre-advent judgment was fulfilled in 1844 when Jesus Christ as our high priest entered into the holy of holies made without hands: the most holy place in the heavenly sanctuary. This special work of pre-advent judgment, which began in 1844, declares to us that all judgment has been given to Jesus and that He who overcame the world is worthy of all honor, glory, and worship. Jesus' high priestly ministry in the holy of holies is the fulfillment of the 2300-day/year prophecy in Daniel 8:14[1] as well as the antitype to ancient Israel's Day of Atonement (Leviticus 23:26-29)—a time of judgment for the people of God (1 Peter 4:17).

Second Angel

"And there followed another [second] angel, saying,
Babylon is fallen, is fallen, that great city, because she
made all nations drink of the wine of the wrath
of her fornication." Revelation 14:8

The book of Jeremiah predicted the fall of ancient Babylon—a prophecy that came to fulfillment when both the city and the kingdom fell to King Cyrus of Persia in 539 BC. In the same literary style as the book of Jeremiah, the second angel's message announces the fall of "Mystery, Babylon the Great, the Mother of Harlots" (Revelation 17:5), which during the time of John the Revelator was a code name for Rome.[2]

History shows us that it was none other than papal Rome that for centuries committed fornication with the kings of the earth (formed a union between the church and the state) and made the nations drunk with her wine (false doctrines and dogmas). The second angel's message came to fulfillment in 1870 when the city of Rome and the remaining Papal States, both of which were under papal control, fell to the king of Italy, thus effectively ending the papacy's temporal rule and power.[3]

Bible prophecy (Revelation 18:1-8) further predicts the final fall of Babylon the Great. She—like her counterpart, ancient Babylon—shall be made wholly desolate during the time of God's fierce judgments (final plagues) upon the earth.

Third Angel

*"And the third angel followed them, saying with a loud
voice, If any man worship the beast and his image, and
receive his mark in his forehead, or in his hand, the same
shall drink of the wine of the wrath of God, which is
poured out without mixture into the cup of his indigna-
tion; and he shall be tormented with fire and brimstone
in the presence of the holy angels, and in the presence
of the Lamb." Revelation 14:9-10*

The third angel's message announces the ominous time in earth's history when those who choose to worship the beast and his image or receive his mark shall drink the cup of God's wrath. God's latter-day people shall face a life-or-death crisis (Revelation 13:15) similar to the crisis that Shadrach, Meshach, and Abed-nego faced: either worship the golden image or die (Daniel 3). For those who refuse to worship the beast and his image and who love not their lives even unto death, the unwavering choice will be clear: "But as for me and my house, we will serve the Lord" (Joshua 24:15).

While the third angel's message has yet to have its fulfillment in history, it should also be pointed out that NO one has the mark of the beast today. Only when the act of worship becomes enforceable upon the world shall the beast's mark of authority (Sunday sacredness) be the test that separates those who worship the beast and his image from those who worship God, the Creator and Lord of the Sabbath (Exodus 20:8-11).

In the time of the third angel's message, there will be a great spiritual awakening upon the earth (Revelation 18:1-3). Proclaimed with great power and glory, the third angel's message, in opposition to the dark trinity's false doctrines and miracles, will effectively bring God's people out of spiritual fornication with Babylon and will bring the great gospel commission to a close, thus marking the end of Jesus' intercession for the repentant sinner. With the last entry in the Lamb's book of life having been judged, it shall be declared, "He that is unjust, let him be unjust still: and he which is filthy, let him be filthy still: and he that is holy, let him be holy still" (Revelation 22:11).

During a short span of time—starting with Jesus' departure from the heavenly sanctuary and ending with His glorious return to earth—the whole world will be caught up in a great trouble (Daniel 12:1). At this time, God's remnant people will have to persevere under the most severe trials (Revelation 14:12), "as silver tried in a furnace of earth, purified seven times" (Psalm 12:6). This time of trouble will also be reflective of Jacob's time of trouble (Genesis 32:24-28): a wrestling of soul with God in prayer until the dawning of the Sun of Righteousness (Jesus' appearing). "Alas! for that day is great, so that none is like it: it is even the time of Jacob's trouble, but he shall be saved out of it" (Jeremiah 30:7).

As for rest of the world—those whose names are not written in the Lamb's book of life—they too will have a most awful and anguishing time to face when God's fierce judgments, the seven last plagues, are poured out without mercy upon the earth (Revelation 14:9-10). This is the wine of God's wrath that the third angel warns us to avoid.

As Christians living in these latter days, let us not easily ignore or lightly cast aside the solemnity of the third angel's message, given our understanding of the historical fulfillment of the first two angels' messages. The final controversy in this great conflict between Christ and Satan will come down to whom we worship. Will our allegiance be to Jesus, who is worthy of all worship, or to Satan, who through a spurious and counterfeit Sabbath day shall one day stealthily bring much of the world under the banner of worshipping him as the promised messiah?

Summary:

The first, second, and third angel's messages of Revelation 14 form God's latter-day message to His people. As divine proclamations of truth, mercy, and justice for all, they should not be ignored, especially since the first and second angel's messages have already had their prophetic fulfillment in earth's history.

The third angel's message will bring forth a great spiritual awakening as well as division upon the earth. At the close of the third angel's message, the great gospel commission will have ended, thus marking the end of man's opportunity for salvation. At that time, the whole world will be caught up in one big trouble. For God's remnant people, it will be the time of Jacob's trouble, whereas for those who rejected the third angel's message, it will be the time of Egypt's trouble in facing God's final plagues.

> *"And at that time shall Michael stand up, the great prince which standeth for the children of thy people: and there shall be a time of trouble, such as never was since there was a nation even to that same time: and at that time thy people shall be delivered, every one that shall be found written in the book [of life]." Daniel 12:1*

Notes:

1. See Appendix B for more details.
2. The early Christians referred to pagan Rome as Babylon. See 1 Peter 5:13.
3. AD 1870 marks the end of Daniel's 1260, 1290, and 1335-day/year prophecies.

Chapter Thirteen

The Final Trumpet

"And they shall see the Son of man coming in the clouds of heaven with power and great glory. And he shall send his angels with a great sound of a trumpet, and they shall gather together his elect from the four winds, from one end of heaven to the other." Matthew 24:30-31

No one knows the time of Jesus' coming, but Jesus did share with His beloved disciples some signs of when the time would be near. "And as he [Jesus] sat upon the mount of Olives, the disciples came unto him privately, saying, Tell us, when shall these things be? and what shall be the sign of thy coming, and of the end of the world?" (Matthew 24:3).

Jesus warned that great troubles and perplexities would take place upon the earth: "And ye shall hear of wars and rumours of wars. . . . For nation shall rise against nation, and kingdom against kingdom: and there shall be famines, and pestilences, and earthquakes, in divers places" (Matthew 24:6-7).

He also warned of the deplorable and increasingly wicked condition of people's hearts: "Then shall they deliver you up to be afflicted, and shall kill you: and ye shall be hated of all nations for my name's sake. And then shall many be offended, and shall betray one another, and shall hate one another. . . . And because iniquity shall abound, the love of many shall wax cold" (Matthew 24:9-12).

Yet another warning from Jesus to be watching out for will be the deception of many: "For many shall come in my name, saying, I am

Christ; and shall deceive many. . . . And many false prophets shall rise, and shall deceive many" (Matthew 24:5-11).

Seeing that Jesus' warnings (signs of the times) are becoming more relevant and more frequent upon the earth today, it makes one wonder: Is the time of great tribulation which was spoken of by the Bible prophets and Jesus now close at hand? "For then shall be great tribulation, such as was not since the beginning of the world to this time, no, nor ever shall be. And except those days should be shortened, there should no flesh be saved: but for the elect's sake those days shall be shortened" (Matthew 24:21-22).

The time of great tribulation will reach its climax with the great and awful day of the Lord: Jesus' coming. The manner in which He will come and the order of events to take place at His coming need not be a mystery to anyone who makes the Bible their stronghold against human reasoning, as well as against Satan's end-time deceptions!

Eight Signs and Times of Jesus' Second Advent

1) He shall return as He left
When Jesus departed from His disciples, He was taken up into the air and faded from their sight in a cloud. In like manner, Jesus shall come in the clouds of glory. "And when he had spoken these things, while they beheld, he was taken up; and a cloud received him out of their sight. And while they looked stedfastly toward heaven as he went up, behold, two men [angels] stood by them in white apparel; which also said, Ye men of Galilee, why stand ye gazing up into heaven? this same Jesus, which is taken up from you into heaven, shall so come in like manner as ye have seen him go into heaven" (Acts 1:9-11).

2) Every eye shall see Him
Jesus' return will not be a secret event or be seen only here and there throughout the world. From the east to the west, every eye will see Him coming with the angelic hosts of heaven. "Behold, he cometh with clouds; and every eye shall see him, and they also which pierced him: and all kindreds of the earth shall wail because of him. Even so, Amen" (Revelation 1:7).

3) The righteous dead shall rise

At Jesus' coming, the righteous dead shall rise from death's sleep and come out of the grave. Having put on immorality, they shall ascend to meet their Redeemer in the clouds. "For the Lord himself shall descend from heaven with a shout, with the voice of the archangel, and with the trump of God: and the dead in Christ shall rise first: Then we which are alive and remain shall be caught up together with them in the clouds, to meet the Lord in the air: and so shall we ever be with the Lord" (1 Thessalonians 4:16-17).

4) The righteous living shall be transformed

The righteous living at Jesus' coming will also be transformed into the likeness of Jesus by receiving a new and glorious body that shall know no decay. This will happen "in a moment, in the twinkling of an eye, at the last trump: for the trumpet shall sound, and the dead shall be raised incorruptible, and we shall be changed. For this corruptible must put on incorruption, and this mortal must put on immortality" (1 Corinthians 15:52-53).

5) The wicked shall be destroyed

Jesus in the fullness of His glory shall as a consuming fire destroy the wicked by the brightness of His coming. For mortal, sinful man cannot stand in the unveiled presence of God's holiness and live! "And then shall that Wicked be revealed, whom the Lord shall consume with the spirit of his mouth, and shall destroy with the brightness of his coming" (2 Thessalonians 2:8). "And the remnant [of the wicked] were slain with the sword of him that sat upon the horse [Jesus]" (Revelation 19:21).

6) The earth shall be laid waste and left desolate

In the aftermath of Jesus' coming, the earth shall be left devastated and covered with the refuse of the dead. "I beheld the earth, and, lo, it was without form, and void; and the heavens, and they had no light. I beheld the mountains, and, lo, they trembled, and all the hills moved lightly. I beheld, and, lo, there was no man, and all the birds of the heavens were fled. I beheld, and, lo, the fruitful place was a [desolate] wilderness, and all the cities thereof were broken down at the presence of the Lord, and by his fierce anger" (Jeremiah 4:23-26).

"Behold, the Lord maketh the earth empty, and maketh it waste, and turneth it upside down, and scattereth abroad the inhabitants thereof" (Isaiah 24:1).

Furthermore, the heavens above shall no longer give their light: "And I beheld when he [the Lamb] had opened the sixth seal, and, lo, there was a great earthquake; and the sun became black as sackcloth of hair, and the moon became as blood; and the stars of heaven fell unto the earth, even as a fig tree casteth her untimely figs, when she is shaken of a mighty wind. And the heaven departed as a scroll when it is rolled together; and every mountain and island were moved out of their places" (Revelation 6:12-14).

7) The devil and his angels shall be bound

Having left their home in heaven, Satan and his angels at Jesus' coming shall be confined to the desolated earth and shut in under the darkness of heaven until the time of the final judgment. "And I saw an angel come down from heaven, having the key of the bottomless pit and a great chain in his hand. And he laid hold on the dragon, that old serpent, which is the Devil, and Satan, and bound him a thousand years, and cast him into the bottomless pit, and shut him up, and set a seal upon him, that he should deceive the nations no more, till the thousand years should be fulfilled: and after that he must be loosed a little season" (Revelation 20:1-3). "And the angels which kept not their first estate, but left their own habitation, he hath reserved in everlasting chains under darkness unto the judgment of the great day" (Jude 6).

8) The righteous shall reside with Jesus in heaven

In the blessed millennium to come, the saints shall spend the thousand-year respite with Jesus in the heavenly city New Jerusalem. It is here in the city of God that the sons and daughters of Zion will find a most beautiful, peaceful, and refreshing place for their joy-filled souls! "Blessed and holy is he that hath part in the first resurrection: on such the second death hath no power, but they shall be priests of God and of Christ, and shall reign with him a thousand years" (Revelation 20:6).

Summary:

We don't have to face the future with fear or uncertainty. Knowing the Bible's warning signs, the manner of Jesus' coming, and the events leading up to and in fulfillment of His return, we may have a stronghold that will not be easily shaken or swept away by the perplexities and tribulations or the devil's grand deceptions yet to come upon our world.

"Let no man deceive you by any means: for that day [the second coming of Christ] shall not come, except there come a falling away first, and that man of sin be revealed, the son of perdition; who opposeth and exalteth himself above all that is called God, or that is worshipped; so that he as God sitteth in the temple of God, shewing himself that he is God." 2 Thessalonians 2:3-4

Chapter Fourteen

The Bright and Morning Star

"And I heard a great voice out of heaven saying, Behold,
the tabernacle of God is with men, and he will dwell
with them, and they shall be his people, and God himself
shall be with them, and be their God." Revelation 21:3

In looking back across the span of human history, it is not hard to see the enormity of horrors, pains, and sorrows that sin has brought upon our fallen world. Humans and nature alike bear witness to the deep and lasting scars left by sin in the form of defects, diseases, disasters, and death. The Scriptures tell us in 1 John 3:8 that before sin entered our primeval world, it was first born in the heart of the devil, also known as Lucifer—the most perfectly created and highly exalted creature in all the universe!

We may never know or fully understand why or how the mystery of sin came to find existence in such a perfect being, let alone in a perfect environment such as the highest of heavens. But one thing is for sure: Sin and sinners have no home in heaven! Having profaned their heavenly sanctuary, both Lucifer and his confederacy of sympathizing angels were cast down like lightning to the newly created earth. Having fully turned away from God's love and forbearance, Lucifer had no more hope for redemption and reinstatement. Full of enmity, he set out looking for a way to strike back against God.

In the newly created world, God saw all that He had made, including man, and it was very good (Genesis 1:31). Created in the image of God, Adam and Eve were given God's blessings of procreation and dominion over the earth. Yet somewhere along the way, Satan, who had access to the sinless pair at the forbidden tree in the midst of the garden of Eden, quickly moved upon his opportunity with Eve alone and stealthily brought about her fall. Adam, who loved Eve as his own flesh, willingly shared in Eve's fate and forfeited his God-given dominion to Satan, the self-proclaimed ruler and dark prince of this world.

We may never know or fully understand why God allowed sin to come into our world, but one thing is for sure: Sin and sinners shall one day be no more! "And the Lord God said unto the serpent, . . . I will put enmity between thee [Satan] and the woman, and between thy seed and her seed; it [Jesus] shall bruise thy head, and thou shalt bruise his heel" (Genesis 3:14-15).

From the time of Adam and Eve's expulsion from their Eden home to the appointed time of the promised Messiah, Satan had a stronghold on both man and nature, including the power (keys) of death. As the promised Messiah, Jesus by His death made atonement for man's sins (transgressions of the Law), regained all that Adam and Eve had forfeited, and cast a deadly wound upon Satan, the serpent of old. Furthermore, Jesus' death affirmed to the universe that God's Law, the law of love, is just, true, and never-ending, even as God is from everlasting to everlasting.

Even more so, Jesus' victory over sin and death is now our victory! "O death, where is thy sting? O grave, where is thy victory? The sting of death is sin; and the strength of sin is the law. But thanks be to God, which giveth us the victory through our Lord Jesus Christ" (1 Corinthians 15:55-57).

With God's promise in Genesis 3:15 fulfilled in Jesus, we can rest assured in Jesus' promises: "I am the resurrection, and the life: he that believeth in me, though he were dead, yet shall he live: and whosoever liveth and believeth in me shall never die" (John 11:25-26). "Let not your heart be troubled: ye believe in God, believe also in me. In my Father's house are many mansions: if it were not so, I would have told you. I go to prepare a place for you. And if I go and prepare a place for you, I will come again, and receive you unto myself; that where I am, there ye may be also" (John 14:1-3).

The blessed hope of every believer and overcomer is to see their Redeemer face-to-face and to experience eternity with Him. "For I know that my redeemer liveth, and that he shall stand at the latter day upon the earth: and though after my skin worms destroy this body, yet in my flesh shall I see God: whom I shall see for myself, and mine eyes shall behold, and not another; though my reins be consumed within me" (Job 19:25-27). Jesus Christ, "the bright and morning star" (Revelation 22:16), shall at His glorious appearing cast away the darkness, call open the graves, and gather from the four corners of the earth His redeemed people. "Beloved, now are we the sons of God, and it doth not yet appear what we shall be: but we know that, when he shall appear, we shall be like him; for we shall see him as he is" (1 John 3:2).

What will heaven be like? What will the sons and daughters of God be doing on the new earth? The truth be told, "Eye hath not seen, nor ear heard, neither have entered into the heart of man, the things which God hath prepared for them that love him" (1 Corinthians 2:9). Words cannot adequately describe the wonders, joys, and discoveries that await those who have overcome Satan and the curse of sin by the blood of Lamb, yet the Scriptures do cast a glimmering light on the saints' future home: the paradise of God.

The New Jerusalem

While Satan and his confederacy of evil angels are bound to the void and desolated earth for a thousand years, the saints shall experience "heaven" in the paradise city of God. In John the Revelator's glorious vision, the holy city, New Jerusalem, is described as follows: "Her light was like unto a stone most precious, even like a jasper stone, clear as crystal" (Revelation 21:11). "For the glory of God did lighten it, and the Lamb [Jesus] is the light thereof" (Revelation 21:23). "And the building of the wall of it was of jasper. . . . And the foundations of the wall of the city were garnished with all manner of precious stones. . . . And the twelve gates were twelve [single] pearls: . . . and the street of the city was pure gold, as it were transparent glass" (Revelation 21:18-21). "And the city lieth foursquare, and the length is as large as the breadth: and he [the angel] measured the city with the [golden] reed, twelve thousand furlongs [about 1,500 miles]. The length and the breadth and the height of it are equal" (Revelation 21:16). "And there shall in no wise enter into it any thing that defileth, neither whatsoever worketh abomination, or maketh a lie: but they which are written in the Lamb's book of life" (Revelation 21:27).

In addition to the resplendent beauty, grandeur, and uncontaminated atmosphere within the holy city's pearly gates, the overcomers (saints) shall grow in stature, wisdom, knowledge, and unity (brotherly love) as they come together each month and partake from the tree of life. "And he shewed me a pure river of water of life, clear as crystal, proceeding out of the throne of God and of the Lamb. In the midst of the street of it, and on either side of the river, was there the tree of life, which bare twelve manner of fruits, and yielded her fruit every month: and the leaves of the tree were for the healing of the nations" (Revelation 22:1-2).

The New Earth

At the end of the saints' blissful millennium, John the Revelator saw the holy city coming down out of heaven and uniting with the earth. "And I John saw the holy city, New Jerusalem, coming down from God out of heaven, prepared as a bride adorned for her husband" (Revelation 21:2). Here is presented New Jerusalem, the bride and wife of the Lamb, coming down out of heaven to meet Jesus, the bridegroom, standing upon the earth. As for the saints (wedding guests), they shall forever share in this holy union between heaven and earth as the precious jewels of the eternal city and as living ornaments on the new earth—our paradise home for all eternity!

In the new earth, the saints shall live out their days of eternity free from the wiles of the great tempter (Satan) and sinners. "And the devil that deceived them was cast into the lake of fire and brimstone. . . . And death and hell were cast into the lake of fire. This is the second death. And whosoever was not found written in the [Lamb's] book of life was cast into the lake of fire" (Revelation 20:10-15). They will also be free from the curse of sin itself. "And God shall wipe away all tears from their eyes; and there shall be no more death, neither sorrow, nor crying, neither shall there be any more pain: for the former things are passed away" (Revelation 21:4).

The saints' work and activities upon the new earth shall not be in vain or looked upon as drudgery. "My people shall dwell in a peaceable habitation, and in sure dwellings, and in quiet resting places" (Isaiah 32:18). "Violence shall no more be heard in thy land, wasting nor destruction within thy borders; but thou shalt call thy walls Salvation, and thy gates Praise" (Isaiah 60:18). "They shall build houses, and inhabit them; and they shall plant vineyards, and eat the fruit of them. They shall not build, and another inhabit; they shall not plant, and another eat: . . . mine elect shall long enjoy the work of their hands" (Isaiah 65:21-22).

Nature itself will be restored to its primeval beauty and grandeur, and all God's creatures will live in harmony with each other. "The wilderness and the solitary place shall be glad for them; and the desert shall rejoice, and blossom as the rose" (Isaiah 35:1). "Instead of the thorn shall come up the fir tree, and instead of the brier shall come up the myrtle tree" (Isaiah 55:13). "The wolf also shall dwell with the lamb, and the leopard shall lie down with the kid; . . . and a little child shall lead them. . . . They shall not hurt nor destroy in all my holy mountain: for the earth shall be full of the knowledge of the Lord, as the waters cover the sea" (Isaiah 11:6-9).

The New Heavens

Not only will the earth be restored to everlasting beauty and harmony, but "the heavens [which] declare the glory of God; and the firmament [that] sheweth his handywork" will also be restored (Psalm 19:1). "For, behold, I create new heavens and a new earth: and the former shall not be remembered, nor come into mind" (Isaiah 65:17).

What are these new heavens? The first will be the firmament or sky above the new earth; the second will be the starry constellations and planets of our renewed galaxy; and the third or highest heaven is, and was, and always will be where God himself resides.

All in all, the glories of the new earth, the new heavens, and the New Jerusalem together shall speak of the untold wonders, joy, peace, and eternal happiness that await the redeemed sons and daughters of God. "And the Spirit and the bride say, Come. And let him that heareth say, Come. And let him that is athirst [after righteousness] come. And whosoever will, let him [come and] take the water of life freely" (Revelation 22:17).

Summary:

The amazing and wondrous things that God is preparing for those who love Him and who thirst after righteousness are truly beyond human comprehension or imagination. For those cleansed and made righteous by the blood of Lamb (Jesus), the new earth, new heavens, and New Jerusalem shall be so truly awesome and glorious to behold and experience that the cares, toils, and sorrows of this sin-sick world will be long forgotten!

"I will greatly rejoice in the Lord, my soul shall be joyful in my God; for he hath clothed me with the garments of salvation, he hath covered me with the robe of righteousness, as a bridegroom decketh himself with ornaments, and as a bride adorneth herself with her jewels. For as the earth bringeth forth her bud, and as the garden causeth the things that are sown in it to spring forth; so the Lord God will cause righteousness and praise to spring forth before all the nations." Isaiah 61:10-11

"Blessed are they that do his commandments, that they may have right to the tree of life, and may enter in through the [pearly] gates into the city [of God]." Revelation 22:14

Epilogue

As a fellow Christian, I believe that God has His people scattered within all the Christian sects. As for the traditions and dogmas among the various Christian sects, it is these things which both define and distinguish us as Roman Catholic, Orthodox, Protestant, Mormon, or Evangelical. I also believe that as Christians, God holds us individually accountable to the truth we have been given under the conviction of the Holy Spirit.

What is truth? The Bible declares to us: "Sanctify them in the truth; Your word is truth" (John 17:17, NASB), and "He [the Holy Spirit of truth] will guide you into all the truth" (John 16:13, NASB). In other words, our faith and Christian beliefs must be built upon the rock of Christ: "So faith comes from hearing, and hearing by the word of Christ" (Romans 10:17, NASB). Anything else, including the traditions of men and the dogmas of religion, "will be like the foolish man who built his house on the sand. The rain fell [heavy sorrows], and the floods came [persecutions], and the winds blew [demonic forces and worldly strife] and slammed against that house [man's spiritual house]; and it fell—and great was its fall" (Matthew 7:26-27, NASB).

As a student of Bible prophecy, I believe that we are living in a most precarious time: "the time of the end" as spoken of by the Bible prophet Daniel. With humanitarian crises (natural and manmade disasters) and worldly strife, as well as humanism and social globalism, all quickening at a rapid pace, it seems as though our world is progressively moving towards some ominous endpoint. Even Christendom as a whole has become deluded to the point where many nominal Christians today can barely distinguish between Bible truth and the enemy's seeds of error sown within our world.

Is the Bible outdated and obsolete for the modern-day Christian? I think not! God's Word, which has endured down through the ages, not only is relevant but is the standard by which all Christian experience and faith must be tested. In His Word we find not only hope for the future but warning and understanding of the subtle lies and schemes of the devil, who in the last days shall attempt to deceive even the very elect—Christians!

My fellow brothers and sisters in Christ, let us heed Jesus' warning (Matthew 24) and the call to put on the whole armor of God (Ephesians 6:10-18) so that we may be able to stand in the evil day against the schemes of the devil. Let us raise up the banner of truth and boldly blow the trumpet to warn others until the everlasting gospel has gone into all the world. Then surely, as is promised by Him who is faithful and true, the end shall quickly come!

> *"Who shall separate us from the love of Christ? shall*
> *tribulation, or distress, or persecution, or famine, or*
> *nakedness, or peril, or sword? . . . Nay, in all these things*
> *we are more than conquerors through him that loved us."*
> Romans 8:35-37

Appendix A

Daniel's Kingdom Prophecies

Kingdom	Daniel 2	Daniel 7	Daniel 8
Babylon (605-539 BC)	Head of gold (verses 32, 38)	Lion with wings (verse 4)	[Daniel's vision pertains to the time when Babylon is already fallen.]
Media-Persia (539-331 BC)[1]	Chest and arms of silver (verses 32, 39)	Bear with one shoulder higher than the other (verse 5)	Ram with one horn longer than the other (verses 3, 20)
Greece (331-168 BC)[2]	Thighs of brass (verses 32, 39)	Leopard with 4 wings and 4 heads (verse 6)	Goat whose large horn is broken off and replaced by 4 horns (verses 5, 8, 21, 22)
Rome (168 BC- AD 476)[3]	Legs of iron (verses 33, 40)	A dreadful and terrifying beast with great iron teeth and 10 horns (verses 7, 19, 23)	A little horn which comes up after the goat's 4 horns, replacing them (verses 9-12, 23-25)
Rome—divided and broken (AD 476 to present)	Feet and toes of iron and clay (verses 33, 41)	10 horns; 3 replaced by another "little" horn (verses 8, 24, 25)	The little horn magnified against the Most High (verses 23-25)
God's kingdom on earth (yet to come)	A stone cut without hands (verses 34, 44)	An everlasting kingdom (verses 18, 22, 27)	The power that shall break without hands the little horn kingdom (verse 25)

---

1. 539 BC: Cyrus' capture of the city of Babylon (some historians put this date at 538 BC)
2. 331 BC: The second and decisive defeat of King Darius at Gaugamela
3. 168 BC: The decisive defeat of the Macedonians at the battle of Pydna

Appendix B

Daniel's Timeline Prophecies

2300-Day and 70-Week Prophetic Timeline	
457 BC	Start of the 2300 days/years and 70 weeks or 490 years (Daniel 9:25)
	Historical event: King Artaxerxes' decree to restore and rebuild Jerusalem
408 BC	End of the 7 weeks or 49-year period (Daniel 9:25)
	Historical event: Ezra and Nehemiah's time of repair to the broken-down walls and streets of the city of Jerusalem
AD 27	Start of the 70th week (Daniel 9:26-27)
	Historical event: Jesus' baptism and anointing by the Holy Spirit
AD 31	Middle of the 70th week (Daniel 9:26-27)
	Historical event: Jews' rejection of the Messiah: Jesus' crucifixion
AD 34	End of the 70th week (490th year)
	Historical event: Jews' rejection of the gospel: the stoning of Stephen
AD 1844	End of the 2300 days (Daniel 8:13-14)
	Historical event: The Great Disappointment (misunderstanding of Jesus' coming into the holy of holies to restore/cleanse the heavenly sanctuary)
	The first angel's announcement (Revelation 14:6-7)

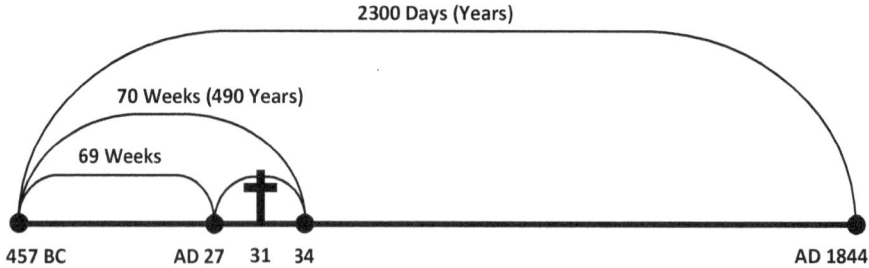

1260, 1290, and 1335-Day Prophetic Timeline	
AD 535	Start of the 1335 days (Daniel 12:12) Historical events: The start of the Gothic Wars; Justinian's Novels were enacted, laying the groundwork for the papacy's rising
AD 580	Start of the 1290 days (Daniel 12:11) Historical event: The taking away of the daily (the dissolution of the Senate—the last remaining branch of government in the city of Rome)
AD 610	Start of the 1260 days (Daniel 7:25, 12:7) Historical event: The setting up of the abomination of desolation in the West (the establishment of the papacy's temporal power in the city of Rome) during the new emperor's troubles in the Eastern Roman Empire
AD 1870	Start of the "Time of the End" (Daniel 12:4, 9) End of the 1260, 1290, and 1335-day/year prophecies Historical event: The papacy's surrender of the city of Rome and the full removal of its temporal power The second angel's announcement (Revelation 14:8)

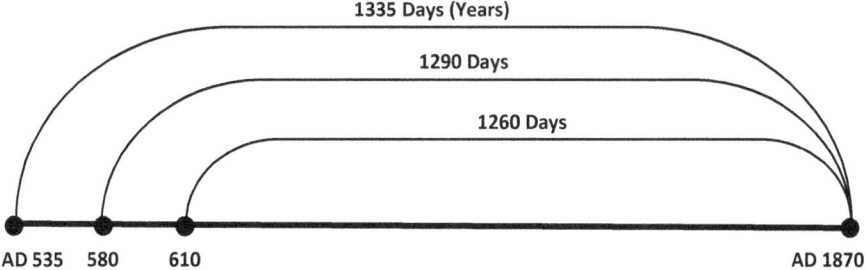

Appendix C

The Millennial Kingdom of God

"After Christ comes, all the peoples of the earth will be subject to him, but there will be multitudes of people on the face of the earth who will not be members of the Church; yet all will have to be obedient to the laws of the kingdom of God, for it will have dominion upon the whole face of the earth. These people will be subject to the political government, even though they are not members of the ecclesiastical kingdom which is the Church. This government which embraces all the peoples of the earth, both in and out of the Church, is also sometimes spoken of as the kingdom of God, because the people are subject to the kingdom of God which Christ will set up; but they have their [free] agency and thousands will not be members of the Church until they are converted; yet at the same time they will be subject to the theocratic rule."[1]

Mormon interpretation of Bible prophecy as well as Mormon doctrine declare that the kingdom of God during the time of Jesus' reign upon the earth (the anticipated millennium preceding the final judgment—Revelation 20:6-15) will be a religious-political kingdom governed by the hierarchy of The Church of Jesus Christ of Latter-day Saints. The religious order—the LDS Church—shall be governed by the "Council of the Church" and the political order—the Kingdom of God—shall be governed by the "Council of Fifty."

The Kingdom of God on Earth

The following outline summarizes the distinctions between the two ruling orders:

The LDS Church (ecclesiastical horn of the kingdom)
- Established April 6, 1830
- Public membership
- Led by the Church's First Presidency and Quorum of Twelve Apostles
- President of the Church is the presiding **high priest** over the "Council of the Church"
- Church leaders are selected by revelation, yet before holding office must be sustained by a general membership vote
- Membership governance: The "Book of Commandments" (Doctrine and Covenants)

The Kingdom of God (political horn of the kingdom)
- Established March 11, 1844
- Private membership
- Led by the "Council of Fifty"
- President of the Church is the presiding **king** over the Council of Fifty
- Council leaders rule by divine appointment, not by election
- Public governance: The "Law of Common Consent" will operate in the political affairs of men

Council of the Church
(Not to be confused with the *Common Council of the Church*)

"In The Church of Jesus Christ of Latter-day Saints, the *Council of the Church* is the supreme governing body of the church which holds the power to make the final decision on any spiritual matter that will affect any member of the church. Its existence and status are uncertain and controversial, and the body has not been formally convened since the presidency of John Taylor. For this reason, few Latter-day Saints have heard of the council or are familiar with its potential powers. However, in the church today, the First Presidency and the Quorum of the Twelve Apostles hold weekly combined meetings in the Salt Lake Temple. This meeting acts in the church as the de facto highest governing council. Thus, the joint meetings of the First Presidency and the Quorum of the Twelve Apostles may be said to be the de facto, if not the de jure, Council of the Church."[2]

"Again, verily, I say unto you, the most important business of the church, and the most difficult cases of the church, inasmuch as there is not satisfaction upon the decision of the bishop or judges, it shall be handed over and carried up unto the *council of the church*, before the Presidency of the High Priesthood. And the Presidency of the council of the High Priesthood shall have power to call other high priests, even twelve, to assist as counselors; and thus the Presidency of the High Priesthood and its counselors shall have power to decide upon testimony according to the laws of the church. . . . This is the highest council of the church of God, and a final decision upon controversies in spiritual matters."[3]

Council of Fifty

"*The Council of Fifty*, a council formed in Nauvoo in 1844, provided a pattern of political government under priesthood and revelation. It was, to its members, the nucleus or focus of God's latter-day kingdom. . . . In this framework, the Council of Fifty was viewed as the seed of a new political order that would rule, under Christ, following the prophesied cataclysmic events of the last days."[4]

Book of Commandments

"In 1833, a number of the revelations received by the Prophet Joseph Smith were prepared for publication under the title *A Book of Commandments for the Government of the Church of Christ*. The Lord continued to communicate with his servants, and an enlarged compilation of revelations was published two years later as the Doctrine and Covenants."[5]

"Behold, this is mine authority, and the authority of my servants, and my preface unto *the book of my commandments*, which I have given them to publish unto you, O inhabitants of the earth."[6]

Law of Common Consent

"Today the Church continues to operate by divine revelation and *common consent*. Callings to positions of Church service at all levels of the organization and ordination to the priesthood are made by the inspiration of authorized leaders and are then brought before the appropriate body of members to be sustained or opposed. Members do not nominate persons to office, but are asked to give their sustaining vote to decisions of presiding councils by raising their right hand, and anyone may give an opposing vote in the same way. This procedure is also followed in accepting important revelations and scriptural additions."[7]

"And all things shall be done by *common consent* in the church, by much prayer and faith, for all things you shall receive by faith. Amen."[8]

An Image (Likeness) to the Beast

George Santayana famously said, "Those who cannot remember the past are condemned to repeat it." If history is any indication of the future, then the declaration to "make an image [likeness] to the beast, which had the wound by a sword, and did live" (Revelation 13:14) may be in reference to a system of governance that is similar to the Roman papacy—the beast that was mortally wounded and did live again.

"There is *the Roman Catholic system*, which believes that it is the kingdom of God on earth and unites both political and religious authority in one [theocratic] system under one head and consequently claims a God-given right to rule in both political and religious realms."[9]

"Theocracy: A form of civil government in which God himself is recognized as the head. The laws of the commonwealth are the commandments of God, and they are promulgated and expounded by the accredited representatives of the invisible Deity, real or supposed—generally a priesthood. Thus in a theocracy civic duties and functions form a part of religion, implying the absorption of the State by the Church or at least the supremacy of the latter over the State."[10]

"The Supreme Pontiff, Sovereign of Vatican City State, has the fullness of legislative, executive and judicial powers."[11]

"Supreme Pontiff Francis: Bishop of Rome; Vicar of Jesus Christ; Successor of the Prince of the Apostles; Supreme Pontiff of the Universal

Church; Primate of Italy; Metropolitan Archbishop of the Province of Rome; Sovereign of the State of Vatican City; Servant of the Servants of God."[12]

The Mormon prophet Joseph Smith envisioned a syncretized system of governance: a theocracy similar to the Roman papacy, but having ideals and principles similar to the democracy of the United States—a theo-democracy.

"As the *world is governed too much*' and as there is not a nation or dynasty, now occupying the earth, which acknowledges Almighty God as their law giver, and as 'crowns won by blood, by blood must be maintained,' **I go emphatically, virtuously, and humanely, for a THEODEMOCRACY, where God and the people hold the power to conduct the affairs of men in righteousness.** And where liberty, free trade, and sailor's rights, and the protection of life and property shall be maintained inviolate, for the benefit of ALL. To exalt mankind is nobly acting the part of a God; to degrade them, is meanly doing the drudgery of the devil. *Unitas, libertas, caritas esto perpetua!* [Unity, liberty, charity in perpetuity!] With the highest sentiments of regard for all men, I am an advocate of unadulterated freedom. JOSEPH SMITH"[13]

To help explain Joseph's theory of theo-democratic governance, former Brigham Young University professor Matthew O. Richardson provides the following comments:

"To better understand common consent, it is important first to understand the workings of the government of God. Elder Harold B. Lee described the government of the kingdom of God as a theocracy but also 'something like a democracy.' This description is a simple clarification of a seemingly complex and often misunderstood organization. Elder Lee highlighted two significant pillars in the Lord's government: theocracy and democracy. The first pillar, theocracy, accents Christ's undeniable position as head of the kingdom—the sole proprietor. The second pillar, democracy, emphasizes the people's opportunity to participate in their government. This combination of terms, however, immediately raises questions from traditional political sciences. How can a theocracy also be described as a democracy? On the surface these terms not only seem incompatible but provoke a jealous power struggle. A democracy doesn't seem to fit with a theocracy because of the world's understanding and definition of democracy. But thankfully, when this term is properly understood, the powerful second pillar not only fits but is seen for the essential principle in gospel government and doctrine it is.

"The pillar of democracy that Elder Lee described in the Lord's kingdom was something *like* a democracy. In a traditional democracy, power is vested in the people and they hold participatory rights. The role of the people under a conventional theocracy, on the other hand, is being part of the kingdom rather than of its governmental process and procedure. The Lord's kingdom, unlike a conventional theocracy, allows the members to participate in its government. This unique combination in which all power is vested in the Lord (theocracy) with the participation of the people (democracy) has thus been called a theo-democracy, which is a form of government in which the decisions for the kingdom of the Lord are His decisions but in which His people have been given the opportunity to exercise their presence in that kingdom. Members of the Lord's kingdom exercise their democratic presence through the principle of common consent."[14]

Notes:

1. Bruce R. McConkie, ed., *Doctrines of Salvation—Sermons and Writings of Joseph Fielding Smith*, vol. 1 (Salt Lake City, UT: Deseret Book, 1954), 141
https://archive.org/stream/Doctrines-of-Salvation-volume-1-2-3-joseph-fielding-smith/JFSDoctrinesofSalvationvFULL#page/n0/mode/2up

2. Wikipedia, "Council of the Church"
https://en.wikipedia.org/wiki/Council_of_the_Church

3. *The Doctrine and Covenants of the Church of Jesus Christ of Latter-day Saints* (Salt Lake City, UT: The Church of Jesus Christ of Latter-day Saints, 1981), 107:78-80

4. *Encyclopedia of Mormonism*, "Council of Fifty"
https://eom.byu.edu/index.php/Council_of_Fifty

5. The Church of Jesus Christ of Latter-day Saints/The Guide to the Scriptures/Book of Commandments
https://www.lds.org/scriptures/gs/book-of-commandments?lang=eng

6. *Doctrine and Covenants* 1:6

7. *Encyclopedia of Mormonism*, "Common Consent"
https://eom.byu.edu/index.php/Common_Consent

8. *Doctrine and Covenants* 26:2

9. J. Dwight Pentecost, *Romanism in the Light of Scripture* (CreateSpace Self-Publishing Platform, 2014), 5

10. James F. Driscoll, *Catholic Encyclopedia*, vol. 14 (1913), "Theocracy"
https://en.wikisource.org/wiki/Catholic_Encyclopedia_(1913)/Theocracy

11. Fundamental Law of Vatican City State, Article 1 (Nov. 26, 2000)
http://www.vaticanstate.va/content/dam/vaticanstate/documenti/leggi-e-decreti/Normative-Penali-e-Amministrative/FundamentalLaw1.pdf

12. Vatican City State
http://www.vaticanstate.va/content/vaticanstate/en/stato-e-governo/struttura-del-governatorato/organigramma/stato-citta-del-vaticano.html

13. Joseph Smith, "The Globe," *Times and Seasons*, vol. 5, no. 8 (April 15, 1844): 510
https://archive.org/stream/TimesAndSeasonsVol5/Times_and_Seasons_Vol_5#page/n217/mode/1up

14. Matthew O. Richardson, "The Law of Common Consent (D&C 26)," in *Sperry Symposium Classics: The Doctrine and Covenants*, ed. Craig K. Manscill (Provo, UT: Religious Studies Center, Brigham Young University, 2004), 134–141.
https://rsc.byu.edu/archived/sperry-symposium-classics-doctrine-and-covenants/11-law-common-consent-dc-26

Appendix D

The Latter-day Saints

The following testimonial is a brief overview and sketch of The Church of Jesus Christ of Latter-day Saints. It is not intended to be all-inclusive or fully decisive in its witness, but it is written as a modern-day Saint would want it told. For more information about The Church of Jesus Christ of Latter-day Saints, visit www.lds.org.

The Plan of Salvation

In our pre-existence as spirit children of heaven (first estate), we all once lived in the full presence and glory of God. As a heavenly family, we were given many wonderful privileges, the greatest of which was the eternal principle of agency (the freedom to choose between good and evil).

> Man was also in the beginning with God. Intelligence, or the light of truth, was not created or made, neither indeed can be. All truth is independent in that sphere in which God has placed it, to act for itself, as all intelligence also; otherwise there is no existence. Behold, here is the agency of man, and here is the condemnation of man.[1]

In order to help us progress more fully and become like our Heavenly Father, an earthly dwelling (second estate) was created by Jehovah (Jesus Christ) with the Father at His side. "In the beginning, the head of the Gods called a council of the Gods; and they came together and concocted a plan to create the world and people it."[2] "The first principles of man are self-existent with God. God himself, finding he was in the midst of spirits and glory, because he was more intelligent, saw proper to institute laws whereby the rest could have a privilege to advance like himself."[3]

The divine purpose in creating the heavens and earth was ultimately for man's benefit and fullness of joy. Adam and Eve as noble spirits were chosen and ordained by God to be the first earthly couple from which the human race would come into existence. When their spirit bodies were given physical bodies of flesh and bone, they were physically created in the image of God, without sin. It was only after Adam and Eve's disobedience to God's command not to eat from the tree of knowledge of good and evil that death came into the world.

As terrible as this physical and spiritual death decree was to the first earthly couple, it also, unbeknownst to them, opened the way for them as well as for us to progress in our fallen state with the opportunity to return home into the presence of our Heavenly Father, having an immortal physical body like God Himself. That way of promise (Genesis 3:15) was offered up in Jesus Christ as the chosen Son and Savior of the world. "Adam fell [sinned] that men might be [mortal]; and men are [mortal], that they might have joy [potential to become like Heavenly Father]. And the Messiah cometh in the fullness of time, that he may redeem the children of men from the fall" (2 Nephi 2:25-26, from the Book of Mormon).

Before Adam and Eve were given physical bodies, the Father called a grand council in heaven and presented His plan for our progression and happiness. At this council we as His spirit children learned that we would have the opportunity to receive physical bodies like our Heavenly Father, but that the whole human race would be under a veil of forgetfulness so that we would not remember our pre-existence, and that we would come to fall (transgressing God's law). In our fallen state, a Savior would be provided for the atonement of men's sins.

As the Father considered whom to send, Jesus Christ as the first-born of heaven and elder brother to Lucifer came forth and presented himself to the Father: "Here am I, send me" (Abraham 3:27, from The Pearl of Great Price). Lucifer also came forward and presented himself to the Father: "Behold here am I, send me, I will be thy son, and I will redeem all mankind, that one soul shall not be lost, and surely I will do it; wherefore give me thine honor" (Moses 4:1, from The Pearl of Great Price). Seeing Lucifer's hidden selfish motive of wanting to take the glory to himself, Jesus replied, "Father, thy will be done, and the glory be thine forever" (Moses 4:2). After allowing both sons to speak, Heavenly Father declared, "I will send the first" (Abraham 3:27).

With Jesus having been chosen as our Savior, Lucifer in anger began to fuel contention among heaven's inhabitants, and soon afterward he led an open rebellion against God. As a result of Lucifer's (Satan's) rebellion, he and the spirits who aligned themselves with him (one-third of the heavenly host) were cast down out of heaven unto the earth (Revelation 12:7-9). For their treasonous act, they are forever without the opportunity of receiving immortal physical bodies like those redeemed by the blood of the Lamb (Jesus Christ).

> The contention in heaven was—Jesus said there would be certain souls that would not be saved; and the devil [Lucifer] said he would save them all, and laid his plans before the grand council, who gave their vote in favor of Jesus Christ. So the devil [Lucifer] rose up in rebellion against God, and was cast down, with all who put up their heads for him.[4]

This is God's plan for man's progression, that through the sacrifice and atoning blood of Jesus Christ, all may have the opportunity to be as God is. After all is said and done and the day of final judgment has come to pass, all in their resurrected state of immortality, from the sons of perdition to the sons of glory unto glory unto glory, shall give acknowledgment that God is just, merciful, and true in all His ways that are from everlasting to everlasting.

> The Plan of Salvation was created by the Father, brought into reality by the atoning sacrifice of his Beloved Son, and facilitated by the gifts of the Holy Ghost. It embraces the Creation, the Fall, and the Atonement, including the Resurrection, and sweeps across all time from the premortal existence to the final state of immortality and eternal life.[5]

Scriptures

The Scriptures, or what are commonly referred to as the "standard works" of The Church of Jesus Christ of Latter-day Saints, consist of:

1) The Bible (Old and New Testaments)
Latter-day Saints view the Bible as a sacred collection of inspired writings containing God's revelations to man, but not without translation errors. "We believe the Bible to be the word of God as far as it is translated correctly."[6] Although Joseph Smith wrote a translation of the Bible from revelations received (Joseph Smith Translation—JST), the official version of the Bible used by the members of the Church is the King James Version (KJV).

2) The Book of Mormon (Another Testament of Jesus Christ)
Along with the Bible, the Book of Mormon is also revered by Latter-day Saints as a sacred collection of inspired writings for the spiritual benefit of mankind. The Book of Mormon is believed to be not a modern book but a modern-day translation of ancient records that were originally scribed on different plates of metal. These plates contained the historical records of the peoples who lived on the North American continent between about 600 BC and AD 400.[7] As for the purity of the translation of the ancient records or "golden plates" in what is today the Book of Mormon, the Prophet Joseph Smith exclaimed, "I told the brethren that the Book of Mormon was the most correct of any book on earth, and the keystone of our religion, and a man would get nearer to God by abiding by its precepts, than any other book."[8]

For Latter-day Saints the Book of Mormon is the keystone of their religion, their doctrine, their testimony, and their witness to the world.

3) The Doctrine and Covenants
The Doctrine and Covenants (D&C) is a compilation of modern-day revelations primarily received by the Prophet Joseph Smith, with the exception of a few additions by his successors in the Church. The revelations themselves, having been received by inspiration, angelic visitations, and visions, outline God's governing principles, covenants, and sacred ordinances for man's salvation and exaltation. The Doctrine

and Covenants contains 138 sections and two official declarations covering the Church's history from September 1823 to June 1978.

> The Doctrine and Covenants is a collection of divine revelations and inspired declarations given for the establishment and regulation of the kingdom of God on the earth in the last days. Although most of the sections are directed to members of The Church of Jesus Christ of Latter-day Saints, the messages, warnings, and exhortations are for the benefit of all mankind, and contain an invitation to all people everywhere to hear the voice of the Lord Jesus Christ, speaking to them for their temporal well-being and their everlasting salvation.[9]

4) The Pearl of Great Price

The Pearl of Great Price is a collected body of selected translations, revelations, and writings by the Prophet Joseph Smith that was first published and circulated in 1851. This five-part collection includes: (1) The Book of Moses, (2) The Book of Abraham, (3) an extract from the Joseph Smith Translation (JST) of the Bible, (4) Joseph Smith's early *History*, and (5) the Church's 13 Articles of Faith. By 1880, this published collection under its current title, "The Pearl of Great Price," was entered into the Church's teachings as a standard work of the Church.

In addition to the Church's recognized standard works, the inspired words of the Church's prophets[10] are also widely accepted by church members as scripture. "We believe all that God has revealed, all that he does now reveal, and we believe that he will yet reveal many great and important things pertaining to the Kingdom of God."[11]

Prophecy and Revelation

The Church of Jesus Christ of Latter-day Saints claims to be Christ's apostolic church once again on the earth, having the fully restored gospel of Jesus Christ. They point out that in the book of Revelation,

> John the Revelator had also foreseen the time when the gospel would be restored. He said, "I saw another angel

(Moroni) fly in the midst of heaven, having the ever-lasting gospel (The Book of Mormon) to preach unto them that dwell on the earth, and to every nation, and kindred, and tongue, and people" (Revelation 14:6).[12]

Another identifying mark of Christ's restored Church upon the earth today is that its members "keep the commandments of God and have the testimony of Jesus Christ," which is the spirit of prophecy (Revelation 12:17; 19:10). The spirit of prophecy in the Church is in general available to anyone who has received the gift of the Holy Spirit after baptism through the laying on of hands by the priesthood authority. The Prophet Wilford Woodruff (fourth president of the Church) wrote, "It is the privilege of every man and woman in this kingdom to enjoy the spirit of prophecy, which is the Spirit of God."[13] Although church members living righteously can receive personal revelation from the Holy Spirit for themselves and their family members, only the president of the Church (who alone holds all the keys of the priesthood) has the presiding authority as a living prophet to receive revelation from God on behalf of the whole Church body.[14]

> If any person should ask me if I [Joseph Smith] were a prophet, I should not deny it, as that would give me the lie; for, according to John, the testimony of Jesus is the spirit of prophecy; therefore if I profess to be a witness or teacher, and have not the spirit of prophecy, which is the testimony of Jesus, I must be a false witness; but if I be a true teacher and witness, I must possess the spirit of prophecy; and that constitutes a prophet; and any man who says he is a teacher or a preacher of righteousness, and denies the spirit of prophecy; is a liar, and the truth is not in him; and by this key false teachers and imposters may be detected.[15]

Joseph Smith

Joseph Smith (Jr.), born December 23, 1805, in the town of Sharon, Vermont, was the fifth (fourth surviving) child of Joseph and Lucy

Mack-Smith. At the age of seven, Joseph suffered from typhoid fever, during which latent complications set in, resulting in a bone marrow infection in his left leg. With the influential help of Dr. Nathan Smith, a physician at Dartmouth College, Joseph's leg was saved from certain amputation using a new yet very painful surgical procedure to remove the infected portion of bone marrow.

During Joseph's recovery, the family moved a short distance to Norwich, Vermont, where after several trying years of farming the family was left poverty-stricken. At age ten, Joseph (Jr.) along with his parents and siblings (five brothers and three sisters) moved to Palmyra, New York. Four years later the family managed to buy a small farm and moved a short distance away to Manchester, New York.

Joseph for the most part was home schooled, but he was aroused to learning about religion by the local religious fervency and revivals taking place among the popular Christian sects in the region, later to be popularly known as the "Burned-Over District" of western New York state. Although his mother and three of his siblings ended up joining the Presbyterian faith, Joseph found himself more partial to the Methodist faith, yet he still hesitated to join with any sect.

> During this time of great excitement my mind was called up to serious reflection and great uneasiness; but though my feelings were deep and often poignant, still I kept myself aloof from all these parties, though I attended their several meetings as often as occasion would permit. In process of time my mind became somewhat partial to the Methodist sect, and I felt some desire to be united with them; but so great were the confusion and strife among the different denominations, that it was impossible for a person young as I was, and so unacquainted with men and things, to come to any certain conclusion who was right and who was wrong.[16]

One day Joseph read from the Bible the inspired words of James 1:5: "If any of you lack wisdom, let him ask of God, that giveth to all men liberally, and upbraideth not; and it shall be given him." Pondering James' words of wisdom, Joseph felt an earnest desire in his heart to know "who of all these parties are right, or, are they all wrong?"[17] He came to the conclusion that he must seek in prayer an answer from God. With faith in one hand and determination in the other, Joseph retreated to the woods behind his family home, where the answer would soon come.

> It was on the morning of a beautiful, clear day, early in the spring of eighteen hundred and twenty. It was the first time in my life that I had made such an attempt, for amidst all my anxieties I had never as yet made the attempt to pray vocally. After I had retired to the place where I had previously designed to go, having looked around me, and finding myself alone, I kneeled down and began to offer up the desires of my heart to God.[18]

In his desire to know the truth, he was first met by the dark, evil forces of the unseen world, but soon afterwards he found himself being delivered from the hands of the Evil One by the visible and audible presence of God the Father and His beloved Son.

> I was seized upon by some power which entirely over-came me, and had such an astonishing influence over me as to bind my tongue so that I could not speak. Thick darkness gathered around me, and it seemed to me for a time as if I were doomed to sudden destruction. . . . Just at this moment of great alarm, I saw a pillar of light exactly over my head, above the brightness of the sun, which descended gradually until it fell upon me. . . . When the light rested upon me I saw two Personages, whose brightness and glory defy all description, stand-ing above me in the air. One of them spake unto me, calling me by name and said, pointing to the other— This is My Beloved Son. Hear Him![19]

Joseph, after regaining his composure, and with the heart's desire to know which of all the Christian sects was the right one to join, asked of God.

I asked the Personages who stood above me in the light, which of all the sects was right . . . and which I should join. I was answered that I must join none of them, for they were all wrong; and the Personage who addressed me said that all their creeds were an abomination in his sight; that those professors were all corrupt; that: "they draw near to me with their lips, but their hearts are far from me, they teach for doctrines the commandments of men, having a form of godliness, but they deny the power thereof."[20]

For the next three years, Joseph and his claim of seeing a vision were met with much skepticism and scoffing by both the local clergy and the area residents. But to Joseph, the vision was undeniably real and without question in his mind. "For I had seen a vision; I knew it, and I knew God knew it, and I could not deny it, neither dared I do it."[21]

On September 21, 1823, Joseph was met with the repeated visitations of an angel named Moroni.[22]

After I had retired to my bed for the night, I betook myself to prayer. . . . While I was thus in the act of calling upon God, I discovered a light appearing in my room, which continued to increase until the room was lighter than at noonday, when immediately a personage appeared at my bedside, standing in the air. . . . He called me by name, and said unto me that he was a messenger sent from the presence of God to me, and that his name was Moroni.[23]

Joseph was instructed by the angel Moroni about a book of golden plates hidden in the earth that contained the historical records of the former inhabitants of the American continent and the fullness of the everlasting gospel as then delivered to the ancient American inhabitants by the Savior (Jesus Christ) after His glorious resurrection. Further instruction was also given to Joseph about a pair of seer's stones and an ancient priesthood breastplate (Urim and Thummim) hidden up with the golden plates for the distinct purpose of translating the ancient records. After repeatedly quoting certain Old and New Testament prophecies soon to be fulfilled (Malachi 3-4; Isaiah 11; Acts 3:22-23; Joel 2:28-32), the angel Moroni departed with a solemn warning to Joseph:

> Satan would try to tempt me (in consequence of the indigent circumstances of my father's family), to get the plates for the purpose of getting rich. This he forbade me, saying that I must have no other object in view in getting the plates but to glorify God, and must not be influenced by any other motive than that of building his kingdom; otherwise I could not get them.[24]

In the years following, while waiting for the commissioned time to receive and translate the golden plates, Joseph while working away from home met and married Emma Hale-Smith (January 18, 1827).

> Immediately after my marriage, I left Mr. Stoal's [Joseph's employer], and went to my father's, and farmed with him that season. At length the time arrived for obtaining the plates, the Urim and Thummim, and the breastplate. On the twenty-second day of September, one thousand eight hundred and twenty-seven [September 22, 1827], having gone as usual at the end of another year to the place where they were deposited, the same heavenly messenger [Moroni] delivered them up to me with this charge: that I should be responsible for them; that if I should let them go carelessly, or through any neglect of mine, I should be cut off; but that if I would use all my endeavors to preserve them, until he, the messenger, should call for them, they should be protected.[25]

With the rampant rumors and speculations of Joseph having a set of golden plates, Joseph for the safety of his family and the plates themselves relocated to his wife's family homestead in Pennsylvania with financial assistance from a respected local farmer, Mr. Martin Harris. Commencing on April 7, 1829, Joseph Smith, along with

Oliver Cowdery as his personal scribe, began to translate the ancient records.

In May 1829, Joseph Smith and Oliver Cowdery were visited by a heavenly messenger, John the Baptist, who came to confer upon them the Aaronic priesthood with the authority to baptize.

> While we were thus employed, praying and calling upon the Lord, a messenger from heaven descended in a cloud of light, and having laid his hands upon us, he ordained us, saying: "Upon you my fellow servants, in the name of Messiah, I confer the Priesthood of Aaron, which holds the keys of the ministering of angels, and the gospel of repentance, and of baptism by immersion for the remission of sins; and this shall never be taken again from the earth until the sons of Levi do offer again an offering unto the Lord in righteousness."[26]

Later on in that same month, near the Susquehanna River (between Harmony, Pennsylvania, and Colesville, New York), both Joseph and Oliver were confirmed with the Melchizedek priesthood authority from three heavenly messengers: Christ's apostles Peter, James, and John.[27]

After the translation was completed in June 1829, groups of three and eight witnesses were shown the golden plates as confirmation of the marvelous work translated by Joseph Smith as God's chosen seer, revelator, and prophet.

Traversing the Midwest with his fellow believers, Joseph continued to spread the teachings of the Book of Mormon while establishing Mormon settlements. Along the banks of the Mississippi River, Nauvoo, meaning "beautiful place," soon became the largest of all the Mormon settlements during Joseph's lifetime.

Joseph often faced ridicule, hostilities, and even physical sufferings along the way. His mission and work abruptly ended when he and his brother Hyrum were murdered by a mob for their faith while incarcerated in the town of Carthage, Illinois (June 27, 1844). His contributions to the Mormon faith continue to live on today in the lives of his fellow believers—the Latter-day Saints.

The Church (Origins and Core Beliefs)

Along with the restoration of the gospel (the Book of Mormon) and the restoration of both the Aaronic and Melchizedek priesthood orders, the time had come for the Church of Christ to be reestablished upon the earth. On the appointed day of April 6, 1830, a group of fifty-some people gathered in the home of Peter Whitmer (Sr.), located in Fayette Township, New York. After prayer and discussion, Joseph Smith was confirmed as first elder, with Oliver Cowdery as second elder of the Church. Altogether six members were ordained that day into the Church, which today bears the name: "The Church of Jesus Christ of Latter-day Saints."

The Prophet Joseph Smith recorded the event as follows:

> [We] made known to our brethren that we had received a commandment to organize the Church; and accordingly we met together for that purpose, at the house of Mr. Peter Whitmer, Sen., (being six in number,) on Tuesday, the sixth day of April, A.D., one thousand eight hundred and thirty. Having opened the meeting by solemn prayer to our Heavenly Father, we proceeded, according to previous commandment, to call on our brethren to know whether they accepted us as their teachers in the things of the Kingdom of God, and whether they were satisfied that we should proceed and be organized as a Church according to said commandment which we had received. To these several propositions they consented by a unanimous vote.[28]

The Church holds to thirteen articles of faith (core beliefs) which its members maintain to be true gospel principles to live by in accordance with the Church's teachings. These articles of faith may be visited at: https://www.churchofjesuschrist.org/study/scriptures/pgp/a-of-f/1?lang=eng

Notes:

1. *The Doctrine and Covenants of the Church of Jesus Christ of Latter-Day Saints* (Salt Lake City, UT: The Church of Jesus Christ of Latter-day Saints, 1981), section 93:29-31

2. Joseph Smith and George Albert Smith, *History of the Church of Jesus Christ of Latter-Day Saints*, vol. 6 (Salt Lake City, UT: Deseret Book, 1950), 308

3. Ibid., 312

4. Joseph Smith, *History of the Church*, vol. 6, 314

5. Daniel H. Ludlow, ed., *Encyclopedia of Mormonism*, vol. 3 (New York: Macmillan, 1992), 1091

6. The Articles of Faith 1:8 (*History of the Church, vol. 4*, 541)

7. *The Book of Mormon: Another Testament of Jesus Christ* (Salt Lake City, UT: The Church of Jesus Christ of Latter-day Saints, 1981), "Introduction to the Book of Mormon"

8. Joseph Smith, *History of the Church*, vol. 4, 461

9. *Doctrine and Covenants*, "Introduction to the Doctrine and Covenants"

10. The LDS Church has always had a living prophet on the earth to guide and direct the Church's affairs, duties, and membership. As of March, 2020, the LDS Church has had seventeen living prophets, the first being the martyred Prophet Joseph Smith.

11. The Articles of Faith 1:9 (*History of the Church*, vol. 4, 541)

12. *Gospel Principles* (Salt Lake City, UT: The Church of Jesus Christ of Latter-day Saints, 1997), 106 (see also *Doctrine and Covenants* 27:5)

13. Wilford Woodruff, "Necessity of the Living Oracles Among the Saints—Exhortation to Obedience to Counsel," *Journal of Discourses*, vol. 9 (April 8, 1862): 324 https://jod.mrm.org/9/324

14. *Doctrine and Covenants* 43:1-7

15. Joseph Smith, *History of the Church*, vol 5, 215

16. Joseph Smith, *Joseph Smith—History* 1:8 (*History of the Church, vol. 1*, 3)

17. Smith, *Joseph Smith—History* 1:10 (*History of the Church*, vol. 1, 4)

18. Smith, *Joseph Smith—History* 1:14-15 (*History of the Church*, vol. 1, 5)

19. Smith, *Joseph Smith—History* 1:15-17 (*History of the Church*, vol. 1, 5)

20. Smith, *Joseph Smith—History* 1:18-19 (*History of the Church*, vol. 1, 5)

21. Smith, *Joseph Smith—History* 1:25 (*History of the Church*, vol. 1, 7)

22. A glorified resurrected being who lived upon the American continent during the degenerate times of the Lamanites and Nephites, according to the Book of Mormon

23. Smith, *Joseph Smith—History* 1:29-33 (*History of the Church*, vol. 1, 10-11)

24. Smith, *Joseph Smith—History* 1:46 (*History of the Church*, vol. 1, 14)

25. Smith, *Joseph Smith—History* 1:58-59 (*History of the Church,* vol. 1, 17-18)

26. Smith, *Joseph Smith—History* 1:68-69 (*History of the Church,* vol. 1, 39)

27. *Doctrine and Covenants* 128:20

28. Smith, *History of the Church,* vol. 1, 75

Appendix E

The Seventh-day Adventists

The following testimonial is a brief overview and sketch of the Seventh-day Adventist Church. As with its counterpart about the LDS Church, it is not intended to be all-inclusive or fully decisive in its witness, but it is equally given as a modern-day Adventist would want it told. For more information about the Seventh-day Adventist Church and faith, visit www.adventist.org.

The Plan of Salvation

In the beginning "the morning stars sang together, and all the sons of God shouted for joy" (Job 38:7), declaring the eternal Father's love to be from everlasting to everlasting. It was here in the glory and beauty of heaven that the Father's love was revealed to all in His planned creation of our world. Yet the Father was not alone in His purposes and plans, for "in the beginning was the Word, and the Word was with God, and the Word was God" (John 1:1). Jesus, the Word, the only begotten and exalted One with the eternal Father, joined with the Father in His plan of creation.

> The Sovereign of the universe was not alone in His work of beneficence. He had an associate—a co-worker who could appreciate His purposes, and could share His joy in giving happiness to created beings. . . . Christ, . . . the only begotten of God, was one with the eternal Father—one in nature, in character, in purpose.[1]

As the second most honored, next to Jesus, Lucifer in his wisdom and beauty as "the anointed cherub that covereth" (Ezekiel 28:14) became jealous of the Father's favor for His Son, Jesus, coveting the glory given Jesus as co-creator. It was here in the heart of Lucifer that the seed of self-exaltation first found its roots, being watered with jealousy and thereafter nurtured with malice towards God Himself. "How art thou fallen from heaven, O Lucifer, son of the morning! . . . For thou hast said in thine heart, . . . I will exalt my throne above the stars of God: I will sit also upon the mount of the congregation . . . : I will ascend above the heights of the clouds; I will be like the most High" (Isaiah 14:12-14).

Filled with the spirit of discontentment, Lucifer left his honored place next to the throne of God and began to sow the seeds of doubt and dissatisfaction among heaven's inhabitants, insinuating that God's governing principles of law and order were unjust and imperfect and were hindering the hosts of heaven from entering into a more exalted, more glorious state of existence. Under a mask of falsehood and deception, Lucifer sought to gain sympathy among the heavenly host by having them question whether Jesus' supremacy and God's authority were for their infinite good and well-being. In doing so, he hoped to secure for himself the allegiance of his sympathizers so that he could bring about a higher order of government where the prerogative of self-exaltation would be a reality and equality with God a possibility. Thus he sought to exalt himself in his own glory, unlike Jesus, who exalted the Father's glory.

> He would never again acknowledge the supremacy of Christ. He had determined to claim the honor which should have been given to him, and take command of all who would become his followers; and he promised those who would enter his ranks a new and better government, under which all would enjoy freedom.[2]

In God's forbearance and unchanging love, which does not demand forced obedience, Lucifer was allowed against the Father's pleadings to continue in his path of rebellion until mercy's appeal was no longer to be heard. As a result of Lucifer's (Satan's) open rebellion and revolt, he and his sympathizers prevailed not and were cast down out of heaven into the earth (Revelation 12:7-9). Realizing the terrible consequences of their irrevocable and treasonous act, Satan and his confederacy of fallen angels soon thereafter began to work out plans for usurping God's purpose and will for the holy pair, Adam and Eve, then residing in the Garden of Eden.

> Satan and those who fell with him were shut out of heaven. . . . Both he and his followers wept, and implored to be taken back into the favor of God. But their sin—their hatred, their envy and jealousy—had been so great that God could not blot it out. It must remain to receive its final punishment. When Satan became fully conscious that there was no possibility of his being brought again into favor with God, his malice and hatred began to be manifest. He consulted with his angels, and a plan was laid to still work against God's government.[3]

Created in the image of God, Adam and Eve had been placed in the Garden of Eden with the blessings of procreation and dominion over the earth. It was here in the garden that the great controversy, which began in heaven, was now to be played out in the sight of the whole universe.

Subject to the same divine law and having the same free moral agency as heaven's inhabitants, Adam and Eve were given free access to the tree of life as long as they lived in obedience to God's law. "Obedience, perfect and perpetual, was the condition of eternal happiness. On this condition he [Adam] was to have access to the tree of life."[4] Satan, having access to the holy couple at the forbidden tree of the knowledge of good and evil, acted upon his devilish plan by sowing in Eve's mind the same subtle lie that he had perpetrated in heaven: "Ye shall be as gods" (Genesis 3:5). Thereafter he brought his plan to fruition through Adam's supreme desire for Eve, which led him to willfully share in her fateful act of disobedience. "Satan exulted in his success. He had tempted the woman to distrust God's love, to doubt His wisdom, and to transgress His law, and through her he had caused the overthrow of Adam."[5]

With the veil of sin now covering the fallen pair and a cloud of sorrow hanging over heaven's inhabitants, Jesus in communion with the Father made known the plan of salvation, which had been laid before the foundation of the world. "God did not ordain that sin should exist, but foresaw its existence, and made provision to meet the terrible emergency."[6] In order to meet man's penalty, Jesus, who had laid the foundations of the earth, would lay down His own life in substitution for the transgressor's life. Adam and Eve, who were to be banished from their paradise home and barred from the tree of life lest they should live on as immortal sinners, were not left without the hope and promise of a Savior (Genesis 3:15).

As Jesus unveiled His earthly mission, the heavenly host were at first saddened in knowing the infinite cost. But as He revealed it more fully, showing that not only would man's redemption be secured but the universe would be forever freed of sin and sinners, the plan of redemption was received with heaven's full acceptance.

> Christ assured the angels that by His death He would ransom many, and would destroy him [Satan] who had the power of death. He would recover the kingdom which man had lost by transgression. . . . Sin and sinners would be blotted out, nevermore to disturb the peace of heaven or earth. . . . Then joy, inexpressible joy, filled heaven."[7]

With paradise now lost, man's redemption fully rested with his Maker, who at the appointed time came into our world. Where Adam fell, Jesus lived a sinless life unto death, so that many should be justified, sanctified, and glorified in Him "who knew no sin: that we might be made the righteousness of God in him" (2 Corinthians 5:21).

> When Adam came from the Creator's hand, he bore, in his physical, mental, and spiritual nature, a likeness to his Maker. . . . Through sin the divine likeness was marred, and well-nigh obliterated. Man's physical powers were weakened, his mental capacity was lessened, his spiritual vision dimmed. He had become subject to

death. Yet the race was not left without hope. By infinite love and mercy the plan of salvation had been devised, and a life of probation was granted. To restore in man the image of his Maker, to bring him back to the perfection in which he was created, to promote the development of body, mind, and soul, that the divine purpose in his creation might be realized—this was to be the work of redemption.[8]

The Son of God came into our world not only to redeem man from the bonds of sin and death but to more fully reveal to the universe God's character, which is as unchangeable as His law—a perfect reflection of His justice, mercy, and love.

But the plan of redemption had a yet broader and deeper purpose than the salvation of man. It was not for this alone that Christ came to the earth; it was not merely that the inhabitants of this little world might regard the law of God as it should be regarded; but it was to vindicate the character of God before the universe.[9]

The Scriptures

Seventh-day Adventists believe the Holy Scriptures (Old and New Testaments) to be the inspired written word of God. Given by divine inspiration through holy men of God who spoke and wrote as moved by the Holy Spirit (2 Timothy 3:16, 2 Peter 1:20-21), "The Holy Scriptures are the supreme, authoritative, and the infallible revelation of His will."[10] Seventh-day Adventists accept the Bible as their rule of faith and practice and hold to the fundamental belief that the Bible should never be studied without prayerfully asking God in faith for the Holy Spirit to guide our understanding of the Scriptures. Following this Biblical premise of study and the principle of interpretation of allowing Scripture to interpret Scripture (Isaiah 28:10), the question, "For what saith the scripture?" (Romans 4:3) is doctrinally answered by Seventh-day Adventists through the Bible's interpretation and not one's own opinion or personal testimony.

In this Word, God has committed to man the knowledge necessary for salvation. . . . They [the Scriptures] are the standard of character, the test of experience, the authoritative revealer of doctrines, and the trustworthy record of God's acts in history.[11]

Prophecy and Revelation

Seventh-day Adventists view the sacred canonical record (Old and New Testaments combined) as a product of the prophetic gift that is sufficient and complete without addition and is to be "the standard by which all teaching and experience [revelation and miracles] must be tested."[12] All divine revelation (visions and dreams) emanates from God the eternal Father and shall always be in full harmony with the Bible.

> The Bible is a perfect and complete revelation. It is our only rule of faith and practice. But this is no reason why God may not show the past, present, and future fulfillment of his word, in these "last days" by dreams and visions, according to Peter's testimony. True visions are given to lead us to God, and to his written word.[13]

As members of the body of Christ continuing the legacy of the Reformation and the Millerite "Advent" movement, Seventh-day Adventists see themselves today in the throes of the great controversy between Christ and Satan. "And the dragon [Satan] was wroth with the woman, and went to make war with the remnant of her seed, which keep the commandments of God, and have the testimony of Jesus Christ," which is "the spirit of prophecy" (Revelation 12:17, 19:10).

> We believe that the prophecy of Revelation 12:17 points to the experience and work of the Seventh-day Adventist Church, but we do not believe that we alone constitute the true children of God—that we are the only true Christians—on earth today. We believe that God has a multitude of earnest, faithful, sincere followers in all

Christian communions, who are true witnesses of the living God in our age.[14]

Believing that all the gifts of the Spirit, including the gift of prophecy, are to remain with "the remnant whom the Lord shall call" (Joel 2:32), and pointing to the "more sure word of prophecy" (2 Peter 1:19-21), Seventh-day Adventists in their understanding of the prophetic books of Daniel and Revelation see themselves in these latter days of the Christian dispensation as being God's prophetic messenger to the world. "The spirit of prophecy is the channel through which the Lord will give instruction, warning, and guidance to the remnant church for the work assigned, and for the preparation required at the second coming of the Lord and Saviour Jesus Christ."[15]

Ellen G. White

Born November 26, 1827, to Robert and Eunice Harmon, Ellen and her twin sister Elizabeth started out life with their six other siblings on a small farm near Gorham, Maine. After several meager years of farming, Robert Harmon, with the hopes of advancing his hat-making business, relocated his family a short distance away to within the city limits of Portland, Maine.

At the age of nine, Ellen's life took a downward turn after she was maliciously struck in the face with a rock by an older female schoolmate. Her physical injuries, which kept her in and out of a state of consciousness, left her after nearly three weeks both emaciated and very much near death. After a lengthy stint of time away from school, she returned, only to find herself struggling to read and write. Because of her chronically poor health, she eventually gave up her dream of becoming a scholar and soon afterwards ceased her formal schooling. "It was the hardest struggle of my young life to yield to my feebleness, and decide that I must leave my studies, and give up the hope of gaining an education."[16]

In March 1840, while attending and listening to William Miller's Advent prophecy lectures in Portland, Ellen came to believe that the Lord's return was close at hand, and yet at the same time she felt unworthy for God to accept her soul into heaven.

> But there was in my heart a feeling that I could never
> become worthy to be called a child of God. . . . Thus
> I wandered needlessly in darkness and despair, while
> they [my Christian friends], not penetrating my reserve,
> were entirely ignorant of my true state.[17]

It wasn't until two years later, after listening to a Methodist camp meeting sermon on justification by faith, that Ellen found release from her feelings and was able to receive without reservation the pardoning love of Jesus as her Savior.

Soon afterwards, at the age of fourteen, she was baptized into the church of her Methodist upbringing. Yet even as a newly baptized Christian, Ellen often felt discouraged, thinking that she must somehow obtain a favorable position with God in order to be rightly accepted into heaven.

> In the Word of God I read that without holiness no man
> should see God. Then there was some higher attainment
> that I must reach before I could be sure of eternal life. I
> studied over the subject continually; for I believed that
> Christ was soon to come, and feared He would find me
> unprepared to meet Him. Words of condemnation rang
> in my ears day and night, and my constant cry to God
> was, What shall I do to be saved?[18]

After much mental anguish over the fearful teaching of an everlasting burning hell for condemned sinners, Ellen's prayerful pleas found God's hand of mercy in a dream where she found herself in the loving presence of Jesus and was given a green cord (symbolizing faith) to hold onto in trusting Jesus for her salvation. As for the heavy burdens covering her soul, they were greatly lifted from her during a public prayer meeting, thus giving her the blessed assurance needed in her conversion experience.

> As I prayed, the burden and agony of soul that I had
> so long endured left me, and the blessing of the Lord
> descended upon me like the gentle dew. I praised

God from the depths of my heart. Everything seemed shut out from me but Jesus and His glory, and I lost consciousness of what was passing around me. . . . My peace and happiness was in such marked contrast with my former gloom and anguish that it seemed to me as if I had been rescued from hell and transported to heaven.[19]

By accepting William Miller's Advent message, Ellen and her family found themselves facing doctrinal differences with their Methodist brethren that ultimately brought them to a crossroads.

When my turn came to speak, I stated the evidences I enjoyed of Jesus' love, and that I looked forward with the glad expectation of meeting my Redeemer soon. . . . Here the class leader interrupted me, saying, "You received sanctification through Methodism, through Methodism, sister, not through an erroneous theory." . . . After leaving the classroom, we [Ellen and her brother Robert] again talked over our faith, and marveled that our Christian brethren and sisters could so ill endure to have a word spoken in reference to our Saviour's coming.[20]

The Methodist minister made us a special visit, and took the occasion to inform us that our faith and Methodism could not agree. He did not inquire our reasons for believing as we did, nor make any reference to the Bible in order to convince us of our error; but he stated that we had adopted a new and strange belief that the Methodist church could not accept.[21]

With Ellen and her family left in the valley of decision, they were summoned to appear before certain members of the church body to answer the charge of walking contrary to the church's rules and teachings. Not willing to yield their faith in the blessed hope of Jesus' soon coming, the Harmon family were quietly disfellowshipped from the church body, and their names were removed from the membership register.

Ellen's high hopes of Jesus' return were cast down to a place of great disappointment in the autumn of 1844, yet she still clung to her belief in Jesus' soon but now delayed coming. It was during this time of perplexity and patience that Ellen's life would meet God's divine calling. In December of that same year, while gathered together in worshipful prayer with four other sisters in Christ, the Spirit of God rested upon Ellen with great power. "While we were praying, the power of God came upon me as I had never felt it before. I seemed to be surrounded with light, and to be rising higher and higher from the earth."[22]

While caught up in vision, Ellen saw the Advent people traveling on a high, straight, and narrow pathway leading to the city of God, New Jerusalem. Behind them was the bright light of the midnight cry message,[23] whereas before them was the illuminated presence of Jesus, who was guiding them onward to the holy city. For some, the city seemed a great distance away, and they began to grow weary, whereas others, denying the light behind them, lost sight of the path and fell back down into the dark and wicked world below. Upon reaching the glorious city, Ellen watched Jesus swing open the city's gate in front of the sea of glass and invite His followers to freely enter. Inside the eternal city she saw the indescribably glorious wonders and splendors waiting for those who have washed their robes in the blood of the Lamb (Jesus Christ).

Not long after her vision, the Lord brought to Ellen's view the trials and troubles that she would have to pass through if found faithful in her calling.

> In my second vision, about a week after the first, the Lord gave me a view of the trials through which I must pass, and told me that I must go and relate to others what He had revealed to me. . . . After I came out of this vision I was exceedingly troubled, for it pointed out my duty to go out among the people and present the truth. . . . For several days, and far into the night, I prayed that this burden might be removed from me, and laid upon some one more capable of bearing it. But the light of duty did not change, and the words of the

angel sounded continually in my ears, "Make known to others what I have revealed to you."[24]

Ever frail and suffering from tuberculosis, Ellen with the help of others managed to share her visions, first with the scattered and discouraged Adventists in Maine and parts of eastern New Hampshire. She was accused of fanaticism and mesmerism by skeptics who looked upon her visions as being anything but from God. An Adventist believer writing to James White said,

> I cannot endorse sister Ellen's visions as being of divine inspiration, as you and she think them to be; yet I do not suspect the least shade of dishonesty in either of you in this matter. . . . I think that what she and you regard as visions from the Lord, are only religious reveries, in which her imagination runs without control upon themes in which she is most deeply interested. . . . I do not by any means think her visions are like some from the devil.[25]

The fact that Ellen was seventeen and had a timid character didn't help matters, but with more and more people desiring to hear Ellen's messages, the harsh voices of skepticism began to slowly wane, surpassed by the favorable testimonies and praises of those who had listened to her messages and had witnessed her in vision. "I can now confidently speak for myself. I believe the work is of God, and is given to comfort and strengthen His 'scattered, torn, and pealed people,'" wrote Captain Joseph Bates.[26]

On August 30, 1846, nearly two years after Ellen's first vision, she married Adventist advocate and minister James White. As newlyweds, they took up residence at the Harmon family home in Gorham, Maine. In the immediate years following, Ellen and James, without a steady means of income, and having to rely on their faith in God's provisions, traveled throughout the northeastern United States to help bring encouragement and unity to the scattered flocks of Adventists, while at the same time reproving the deceptive errors of fanaticism and other erroneous teachings.

Prompted by a vision received in November 1848, Ellen and her husband stepped out again in faith and began to publish a little paper called *Present Truth*—a guidepost to the Creation Sabbath, the heavenly sanctuary, and the third angel's message of Revelation 14.

> After coming out of vision, I said to my husband: "I have a message for you. You must begin to print a little paper and send it out to the people. Let it be small at first; but as the people read, they will send you means with which to print, and it will be a success from the first. From this small beginning it was shown to me to be like streams of light that went clear round the world."[27]

Along with their publishing ministry, they continued to travel, using the meager finances they had, but for Ellen the greatest sacrifice of all was leaving their two young children (Henry and James "Edson") in the care of others while they traveled.

In the summer of 1851, the Whites' publishing ministry was relocated to Saratoga Springs, New York, which not only brought their family back together but opened the way for Ellen's first book to be published: *A Sketch of the Christian Experience and Views of Ellen G. White*. Yet, feeling the pressures of traveling and trying to maintain the publishing work, James White saw the need for Adventists to have their own printing press. On March 12, 1852, a special conference was held, where the decision was made for a printing press to be purchased and owned by an organized body of Sabbath-keeping Adventists. Soon afterwards, the Whites' publishing work relocated to the newly formed Review publishing office in Rochester, New York.

The next few years brought many difficulties and sorrows to the White family, including a heavy debt load and the failing health of James's overworked body. No longer able to bear the load, he turned over the daily responsibilities and finances of the Review office to the Adventist brethren in Battle Creek, Michigan. In the spring of 1861, the Advent Review office was reorganized and incorporated as the Seventh-day Adventist Publishing Association.

While residing in Battle Creek, Michigan, Ellen and her family faced the tragic loss of two of her four sons: Herbert, less than three months old, and her eldest son, Henry, who died almost three years later (December 8, 1863).

> In 1860 death stepped over our threshold, and broke the youngest branch of our family tree. Little Herbert, born Sept. 20, 1860, died December 14 of the same year. When that tender branch was broken, how our hearts did bleed none may know but those who have followed their little ones of promise to the grave. But oh, when our noble Henry died, at the age of sixteen—when our sweet singer was borne to the grave, and we no more heard his early song, —ours was a lonely home.[28]

After the death of her beloved husband, James (August 6, 1881), Ellen decided to remain unmarried the rest of her life. Faithful to her prophetic calling, she did not allow tragedy, hardships, or the frailties of her own life to discourage or deter her from uplifting others and pointing them to Jesus, whom she dearly loved. Altogether her public ministry spanned 70 years and included missions throughout the U.S., Europe, and Australia.

Even after her death (July 16, 1915), her many writings and counsels to the Church have continued to provide hope, comfort, and direction to those seeking a heavenly home. For Seventh-day Adventists, the "Spirit of Prophecy" writings of Ellen White are a lesser light pointing to the greater light: the Word made flesh who is the guiding light of this world.

The Church (Origins and Core Beliefs)

The day following the Great Disappointment of October 22, 1844, Hiram Edson and a few other disheartened Millerites gathered together and began to pray for heaven's light to be shed upon their understanding of the Scriptures so that they could understand the reason for the delay in Christ's coming. Later on that same day, while walking across his cornfield and pondering the Scriptures, a view of Christ opened up upon Hiram's mind in which he saw Jesus Christ as high priest pass from the holy into the most holy place.

> And I saw distinctly and clearly, that instead of our High Priest coming out of the Most Holy of the heavenly sanctuary to come to this earth on the tenth day of the seventh month, at the end of the 2300 days, He for the first time entered on that day the second apartment of that sanctuary; and that He had a work to perform in the most holy before coming to this earth.[29]

After a methodical study of the sanctuary question and the book of Hebrews, Edson and a few others close to him concluded that their understanding of the timing of the 2300-day prophecy (Daniel 8:14) was indeed correct, but that Jesus Christ as high priest had, in antitype to the Jewish Day of Atonement (Judgment), entered into the most holy place of the heavenly sanctuary. Having found a biblical answer to his disappointment, Edson soon afterwards published his findings in an Adventist periodical, *The Day Dawn*.

For retired sea captain Joseph Bates, who had given much of his financial means and tireless energy to the Millerite movement, his disappointment was also met with discovery. Having thoroughly investigated the practice of some Adventists who were then keeping the seventh-day Creation Sabbath, and finding no Scriptural basis for Sunday sacredness, he decidedly began to keep the Sabbath of the Lord and began to publish and preach on the subject. While Bates was preaching about the seventh-day Sabbath at an Adventist conference in Port Gibson, New York, Hiram Edson excitedly saw and shared the biblical link between the Sabbath day, God's Law (the Ten Commandments), and Jesus' high priestly work in the most holy place of the heavenly sanctuary.

Another link to come into Adventist thinking, which would later become a doctrinal belief, was the biblical view of man's state of being after death.

> We, as Adventists, have reached the definite conclusion that man rests in the tomb [void of consciousness] until the resurrection morning. Then, at the first resurrection (Rev. 20:4, 5), the resurrection of the just (Acts 24:15), the righteous come forth immortalized, at the call of

Christ the Life-giver. And they then enter into life ever-lasting, in their eternal home in the kingdom of glory. Such is our understanding.[30]

In addition to the belief in Jesus' premillennial second coming, the links of the heavenly sanctuary, the Sabbath, the state of the dead, and the spiritual gift of prophecy would bring together and forever set apart this small band of post-Millerite Adventists as a peculiar people of the Christian faith.

From 1848 to the time leading up to their formal organization, a series of Sabbatarian conferences were held in the northeastern and midwestern states for the distinct purpose of bringing unification to Adventist thinking, as well as providing an outreach platform for other searching Adventists. On October 1, 1860, at a general confer-ence held in Battle Creek, Michigan, the name "Seventh-day Adven-tist" was adopted. The following October, the Michigan Conference of Seventh-day Adventists was formed, which soon led to other state conferences being formed. Finally, on May 21, 1863, 125 churches, with a membership of 3,500, joined to form the General Conference of Seventh-day Adventists, with John Byington voted in as the first General Conference president.

Holding to the Holy Scriptures as the only rule of faith and prac-tice, Seventh-day Adventists live by the tenets of their faith as set forth in the immutable Word of God. Their fundamental beliefs, 28 in all, outline the Christian life and experience of salvation in Jesus, as well as the duty of each baptized member, as a disciple of Jesus Christ, to be a living witness of the gospel to the world, as fully expressed in one's love for God and fellow man. These 28 fundamental beliefs may be visited at: https://www.adventist.org/beliefs/fundamental-beliefs/

Notes:

1. Ellen G. White, *Patriarchs and Prophets* (Published jointly by Review and Herald Publishing Assoc. and Pacific Press Publishing Assoc., 1890), 34

2. White, *Patriarchs and Prophets*, 40

3. Ellen G. White, *Early Writings* (Published jointly by Review and Herald Publishing Assoc. and Pacific Press Publishing Assoc., 1882), 146

4. White, *Patriarchs and Prophets*, 49

5. Ibid., 57

6. Ellen G. White, *The Desire of Ages* (Oakland, CA: Pacific Press Publishing Assoc., 1898), 22

7. White, *Patriarchs and Prophets*, 65

8. Ellen G. White, *Education* (Oakland, CA: Pacific Press Publishing Assoc., 1903), 15-16

9. White, *Patriarchs and Prophets*, 68

10. Fundamental Beliefs of Seventh-day Adventists
https://www.adventist.org/beliefs/fundamental-beliefs/god/holy-scriptures/

11. Ibid.

12. Fundamental Beliefs of Seventh-day Adventists
https://www.adventist.org/beliefs/fundamental-beliefs/church/the-gift-of-prophecy/

13. James White, "A Test," *Review and Herald*, vol. 7, no. 8 (Oct. 16, 1855): 61
http://documents.adventistarchives.org/Periodicals/RH/RH18551016-V07-08.pdf

14. General Conference of Seventh-day Adventists, *Seventh-day Adventists Answer Questions on Doctrine* (Washington, DC: Review and Herald Publishing Assoc., 1957), 187

15. Arthur G. Daniells, *The Abiding Gift of Prophecy* (Mountain View, CA: Pacific Press Publishing Assoc., 1936), 169

16. Ellen G. White, *Testimonies for the Church*, vol. 1 (Mountain View, CA: Pacific Press Publishing Assoc., 1948), 13

17. Ibid., 14-15

18. Ibid., 23

19. Ibid., 31

20. Ibid., 37

21. Ibid., 41

22. Ibid., 58

23. The "midnight cry," as it came to be known, was a message of warning about Christ's soon coming proclaimed by the Millerites in the late summer and autumn of 1844.

24. White, *Testimonies for the Church*, vol. 1, 62

25. James White, *A Word to the Little Flock* (Brunswick, ME: James White, 1847), 22

26. Ibid., 21

27. Ellen G. White, *Life Sketches* (Mountain View, CA: Pacific Press Publishing Assoc., 1915), 125

28. Ibid., 165-166

29. Quoted in Jerome L. Clark, *1844: Religious Movements*, vol. 1, 67

30. *Questions on Doctrine*, 520

Appendix F

Additional Resources

Latter-day Saint Resources:
Search These Things Diligently: A Personal Study Guide to the Book of Mormon
Brian D. Garner, ©2003, Deseret Book Company, Salt Lake City, UT

Teachings of Prophet Joseph Smith
Joseph Fielding Smith, ©2006, Deseret Book Company, Salt Lake City, UT

Teachings of Presidents of the Church: Brigham Young
The Church of Jesus Christ of Latter-day Saints, ©1997, Salt Lake City, UT

Our Heritage: A Brief History of The Church of Jesus Christ of Latter-day Saints
The Church of Jesus Christ of Latter-day Saints, ©1996, Salt Lake City, UT

Church History in the Fullness of Times
The Church of Jesus Christ of Latter-day Saints, ©1989, Salt Lake City, UT

Building the Kingdom: A History of Mormons in America
Claudia L. Bushman and Richard L. Bushman, ©2001, Oxford University Press, NY

Seventh-day Adventist Resources:
A Brief History of Seventh-day Adventists, 2nd Ed.
George R. Knight, ©2004, Review and Herald Publishing Association, MD

Adventism in America
ed. Gary Land, ©1998, Andrews University Press, MI

The Reformation and the Advent Movement
W. L. Emmerson, ©1983, Review and Herald Publishing Association, MD

Ellen White: Woman of Vision
Arthur L. White, ©1982, Review and Herald Publishing Association, MD

Believe His Prophets
Denton Edward Rebok, ©1956, Review and Herald Publishing Association, MD

Our Paradise Home
S.H. Lane, ©1903, Review and Herald Publishing Association, Washington, D.C.

Subject Resources:
"The Rise of 19th Century American Spiritualism, 1854-1873"
Journal for the Scientific Study of Religion, Vol. 49, Issue 2, pp. 361-33, June 2010
http://onlinelibrary.wiley.com/doi/10.1111/j.1468-5906.2010.01515.x/full

Modern Spiritualism: A Subject of Prophecy and a Sign of the Times, Uriah Smith ©1896
http://archive.org/details/modernspirituali27197gut

History of Spiritualism: http://spirithistory.iapsop.com

God and the People: Theodemocracy in Nineteenth-Century Mormonism
https://academic.oup.com/jcs/article/53/3/349/1022651/God-and-the-People-Theodemocracy-in-Nineteenth

The Political Agenda of the Mormon Church
http://www.janishutchinson.com/agenda.html

CPSIA information can be obtained
at www.ICGtesting.com
Printed in the USA
BVHW042000230420
578043BV00024B/379